Rome and its Empire

THE EXPERIENCE OF ARCHAEOLOGY
Series editor: Andrew Wheatcroft

ROME
and its
EMPIRE

Stephen Johnson

R

ROUTLEDGE
London and New York

First published in 1989 by Routledge
11 New Fetter Lane, London EC4P 4EE
29 West 35th Street, New York, NY 10001

© 1989 Stephen Johnson

Typeset by Columns of Reading
Printed in Great Britain by
T.J. Press (Padstow) Ltd, Padstow, Cornwall

British Library Cataloguing in Publication Data
Johnson, Stephen, *1947–*
Rome and its Empire
1. Roman Empire antiquities
I. Title
937

Library of Congress Cataloging in Publication Data
Johnson, Stephen, 1947–
Rome and its Empire
1. Rome—Antiquities. I. Title.
DG77.J64 1989   937   88–32336
ISBN 0–415–03267–9

Contents

List of illustrations

Acknowledgements

The author and publishers record their thanks to the following institutions and individuals who gave permission for the use of illustrations for this book.

Ashmolean Museum, Oxford, Figure 16
Cambridge University Collection of Aerial Photographs, Figures 10, 28, 29 and 31
Amanda Claridge, Figure 33
English Heritage, Figures 24 and 25
Illustrated London News, Figure 7
Instituut voor Pre-Protohistorie, Amsterdam, Figure 14
Musée de Nîmes, Figures 1 and 21
Museum of London, Figure 13
Newcastle Central Library, Figure 4
Oxford University Press and R.P. Wright, Figure 19
Rheinisches Landesmuseum, Trier, Figures 23 and 39
Royal Commission for the Historical Monuments of England, Figure 6
Saalburg Museum, Bad Homburg, Figures 8 and 26
Society of Antiquaries of London, Figures 11 and 36
André Tchernia, Figure 34
Vindolanda Trust, Figure 15
West Yorkshire Archaeology Service

I am also grateful to Peter Dunn, for providing artwork for the line drawings at Figures 2, 3, 9, 12, 18, 19, 20, 22, 30, 32, 35, 37, and 38, and to Frank Gardiner for supplying the artwork for Figure 25.

Introduction

What is the most enduring impression of the Roman Empire? For some people it may be to gaze with admiration on buildings like the Colosseum at Rome or the Pont du Gard near Nîmes. Others may be more struck by the poems of Virgil or Catullus, or may better appreciate the exploits of historical figures like Julius Caesar or Constantine the Great. Others still may marvel at the historical process through which a small Italian city-state became a major power, first in Italy, then increasing its influence until eventually it imposed its dominance on its known world.

From an archaeological point of view, the most spectacular impressions of Rome are in those sites and buildings where the grandeur can still be appreciated, and where the visitor can feel a close experience of Roman life and civilization. Such places are Pompeii, Lepcis Magna, Timgad, or Piazza Armerina. A more day-to-day reality, especially for those whose normal experience is with the Roman past of an outlying area of Europe only relatively briefly annexed by Rome as one of her minor and most troublesome provinces, is to see and handle familiar pottery, coins, sculptures, mosaics, and other items of daily life displayed in local or national museums, or to appreciate what are normally far more fragmentary remains of Roman buildings and archaeological sites.

Historically, the Romans have had a good press. Their reputation for building solid projects of engineering was such that it was at one time considered that they, and they alone, of the past inhabitants and occupiers of Britain, could have built structures like Stonehenge and other stone circles now known to date from two or three millennia before the Romans arrived. Whilst we know better than this now about the stone circles, the Roman reputation lives on: recent controversy has flared over the 'Roman' road at Blackstone Edge, in the British Pennine Hills near Manchester. The road ascends a one-in-three slope and is formed of a well-metalled pavement with a central groove (for the brakes of carts?) and side ditches. It is still a matter of genuine debate whether such a road was built by the Romans or whether it was one of the earliest turnpike roads of the eighteenth century. There seem few other candidates for its builders.

Within Europe it is difficult not to be aware of the legacy of Rome.

1

Many of the words in use, educational and legal systems, and cultural achievements of many kinds, if they are not derived immediately from classical models, spring ultimately from this underlying source. Periodically architectural designs, buildings, or patterns from the classical world have been rediscovered, and this has led to conscious attempts to reproduce themes or ideas in art or architecture found in ancient material. Some objects from the classical world have never been lost, and have survived since the end of classical antiquity itself. Examples of these are manuscripts collected by the Carolingian court in the eighth and ninth centuries, gemstones and jewellery which were used to beautify bookcovers and other precious objects, and items of artistic value of all kinds, from the ivories now held in cathedral treasuries to pieces such as the Portland Vase. From time to time, such objects have been actively sought. It is due to the respect with which they have been treated – particularly in the case of manuscripts – that so many of the writings from the ancient world have been transmitted to the present day. First of all they were passed on via late Roman scholars, then through library collections, split up and finding their way into late Roman and Carolingian monasteries. From there they were copied and dispersed into other medieval collections until collated by scholars, who have used them to provide standard texts of the ancient authors by a process of textual detective work and criticism.

More obvious perhaps as survivals from the Roman world are the buildings which have never ceased to be visible to those who could travel to see them. Such structures as the Colosseum, the Pont du Gard, and the Porta Nigra at Trier have survived partly by chance, partly through their adaptation in following centuries to different uses, and partly, more recently, as a result of a more enlightened appreciation of what they are and modern concern to retain them. The periodic rediscovery in the past of landmarks such as these by men in a position to influence and lead the tastes of society has ensured that their architectural style is established as part of the familiar, solid background of the landscapes and townscapes of today.

Thus in one sense the archaeology of the classical world has never been lost. It forms part of the accepted cultural backdrop to western civilization, and is in the European subconscious; it is already part of everyday experience. What does require a fresh experience is our new assessment of Roman civilization in all its aspects – a continuous reappraisal of how the Roman empire worked in economic, social, and hierarchical terms, how such a disparate grouping of Mediterranean and Celtic peoples was formed into an amalgam of cultural styles within separate Roman provinces, and what the reality of the empire meant to the individual at different social levels. It is questions such as these, and a host more like them, that the study of Roman archaeology seeks to address.

Figure 1 The Pont du Gard, near Nîmes; part of the aqueduct system bringing water to the city, probably dating from around 20–16BC

The process of rediscovery of the Roman world of which this all forms a part has been a long one. Much of the western European tradition is moulded to a very large degree on the framework set by classical civilizations and sometimes its influence has been hidden, at other times more obvious. Archaeology as a discipline is somewhat younger, but it has as its source the desire to learn more about the past. Thus it is appropriate to start with the Roman period itself in tracing the part archaeology has played, first in feeding off, and later beginning to form, the consciousness of the Roman past.

1

Early archaeology:
before the eighteenth century

Archaeology as a discipline did not begin in earnest until the later
nineteenth or the twentieth century, but the first awakening of an
archaeological interest, provoked by a knowledge of and respect for the
remains of man's past structures and achievements dates from long before
this. Although some signs that the Romans themselves valued the
remains of their own past can be recognized, in general the Roman world
was too involved in self-creation and shaping its own environment to have
much time for the study of buildings and monuments of a bygone age.
Historians such as the emperor Claudius who wrote a compendious study
of the Etruscans, the writers of guide-books (though only describing the
sights of Greece) like Pausanias in the second century, and technical
writers like Pliny were the exception to this rule.

Rome and its origins, however, were perennial subjects of interest as
soon as the empire began to become established and could afford to be a
little more introspective. Writers like Virgil began to glorify and expand
on the mythology of the origins of Rome, spurred on by the splendour of
the Augustan world they saw around them. There were already some aids
to the memory of past events: the rostra, for example, the speakers'
platform in Rome, was so called from the prows of ships originally
exhibited there after the Roman victory at the battle of Antium in 338BC.
Temples, too, acted in a way similar to present-day museums. They were
often cluttered with the spoils of war, votive offerings, and dedications of
captured trophies – the sort of museum which houses a farrago of
curiosities with a hint of regimental splendour thrown in. On the
individual scale, the collection of art treasures was also popular. Artists
sought to satisfy the appetites of the well-to-do for recognized
masterpieces of Greek sculpture by reproducing well-known subjects or
themes after the manner of the originals.

Buildings fared less well. In the later period, at any rate, there seems to
have been no compunction about pulling down old structures to build
new, and many an elegant frieze dating from earlier periods can be found
chopped up and re-used within the core of another, sometimes
considerably less prepossessing structrure. There are some instances,
however, of a more thoughtful approach. For example, Hadrian

4

and northern Italy, by Bramante and Palladio among others. The rediscovery of this classical tradition within Italy soon led to widespread adoption throughout the rest of Europe: by the 1550s it was well established in France, and by the beginning of the seventeenth century it had also become implanted in England through the influence of Inigo Jones, who built the Queen's House at the Palace of Greenwich in the Italian classical style for Queen Anne, the consort of James I of England.

Despite this imitation, the major monuments of the Roman past at the heart of Rome which had inspired it survived only in a poor state and by accident. Those buildings which had escaped despoliation and robbing of their sculpture in order to make lime for the mortar for other buildings during the immediate post-classical period had soon fallen victim to the Saracens who captured Rome in 846–7. An earthquake which severely damaged the Colosseum and partially ruined St Peter's contributed to the decay. By the thirteenth to fifteenth centuries, the zone of the city which comprised the Roman forum had become known as the 'field of towers', because of the multiplicity of domestic fortifications built in the area by rival families. The Arch of Severus was built into one of these fortresses, and the Arch of Titus survives, at least partly, because it formed the entrance arch to another. Further destruction occurred during the course of the fifteenth and sixteenth centuries, despite the concern of men such as Raphael, who counselled Pope Leo X in 1518 that the monuments of antiquity should be preserved and reconstructed where possible. The forum area was steadily becoming buried under the build-up of spoil from other buildings, and suffering from other developments still taking place on its site.

The collecting of antiquities still engendered great interest, and the search for them was keenest in Italy, Professional dealers began to emerge, and in some areas excavations took place to locate antiquities and treasures. This was often accompanied by the destruction of those items which the finders considered worthless or unsaleable. Forgeries were relatively common, and it was not unknown for artists to be commissioned to copy antique statues so that they could be passed off as the genuine article. False inscriptions, or the names of famous men or women from antiquity, would sometimes be added to portrait busts in an attempt to give them a genuine provenance or greater rarity value. The main aim was the exploitation of the Roman past for beautiful objects or treasures, not the increase of knowledge of the Roman world to which they belonged.

Interest was also awakening in the Roman past in areas other than Italy and Rome. Hadrian's Wall, in Britain, had been described within the context of his *Ecclesiastical History of the English People* by the Venerable Bede in the seventh century, but it was not until the sixteenth that antiquarian and scientific interest really began to be aroused. Leland had been appointed 'King's Antiquary' to King Henry VIII, the first and last holder of this post. He made a visit to the wall area in 1539, and his description of its main features makes it clear that he had recognized the wall, its ditch and the vallum, the earthwork which runs to its south for virtually the whole of its length. He also remarked, even at that date, that there was little trace left of the wall in the more populous areas near Newcastle and Carlisle, where the stones had been taken for other buildings. He was followed by other antiquaries, but primarily by William Camden, whose work *Britannia,* in editions published in 1600 and 1607, contains material gleaned from his visit to the wall in 1599. There is no record of any excavation or survey of the remains taking place at this early date, and the wall had to wait about a century for scholarly interest to build up, mainly as a result of the translation of Camden's *Britannia* from Latin, in which he wrote it, into English in 1695. Meanwhile the year 1572 had seen the foundation of a Society for the Preservation of National Antiquities, a clear sign that there was concern about the state of monuments in the country, but this society was disbanded on the accession of James I to the throne of England as being too political.

Recognition of other Roman frontiers had begun on the continent. Collectors of inscriptions and manuscripts had already begun to seek out the places where inscriptions were to be found, and discoveries such as the Peutinger Table, the late Roman map first found in the fifteenth century, gave a new impetus to topographical study. Johannes Turmair, known as 'Aventinus', wrote a historical work in the early part of the sixteenth century in which he mentioned the Roman frontier in southern Germany, identifying it, as he thought, from its traces on the ground. In fact, what he recognized was a road, but his assumption that it was of Roman date, and the suggestion, based on a study of literary sources, that it was built by the emperor Probus (AD272–6) influenced the direction of thinking and research on the frontier for many years.

It was not until the beginning of the eighteenth century that further studies of the German frontier began to appear. The greatest of these, written by the man who is generally considered to have been the 'father of Roman frontier studies in Germany', Johann Alexander Döderlein, appeared in 1723. He recognized that the 'Devil's Wall' was in fact Roman, was able to suggest where it lay on the ground, and predicted that it would be found to have towers. As yet, there was still no systematic excavation to research into questions of the shape and structure of the wall, or the frontier. These were not addressed until the nineteenth century.

Elsewhere, travellers were exploring even further afield. One of the earliest goals for the British was Palmyra, known as Tadmor, which was reached in 1678 by Dr Huntington and others from the English merchant base in Aleppo. This first visit was a disaster, for the travellers found the of his researches into the wall has had to be reconstructed from various editions of the *Handbook to the Roman Wall* written during the nineteenth century by Collingwood Bruce.

Interest in other Roman frontiers was growing apace. By the early decades of the nineteenth century, much research was taking place on the German Odenwald frontier, under the influence of newly established local antiquarian societies. Excavations which were undertaken, however, were still largely unsystematic and uncoordinated; understanding of the results was only partial, and there was often insufficient funding to carry work to a successful conclusion. Nor were there any agreed excavation techniques or objectives, though in southern Germany at least there was a better understanding of the nature of the frontier and the discovery and positioning of watch-towers as part of it. It became clear that in order to plan the work on the German frontier properly, it would be necessary to institute a full research programme with specific objectives.

The first congress of the German historical and antiquarian societies was held in Mainz in 1852. Out of that came the decision to set up a 'commission for research on the Imperial Roman frontier'. Among its stated aims was the need to concentrate and co-ordinate the various activities in the area of the *limes*, and to ensure not only that the work was systematized, but also that it should only be carried out by those qualified to do so. Despite these high ideals, much of the work in individual areas of the frontier was still left to local initiatives, and there was little or no support funding for the task from central reserves.

The appointment of Theodor Mommsen, an exceptional scholar and historian, as president of the commission in 1872 led to a far greater thoroughness and the formulation of a research strategy which could be expected to bear fruit. He appointed a team of historians and archaeologists, who, with the support of amateur enthusiasts, were to attempt within a five-year programme to reveal the history of the frontier through an excavation campaign directed towards the *limes* itself, its component structures and watch-towers, and the majority, if not all, of the forts. The *limes* was divided into fifteen sections, each of which was overseen by a *kommissar* who directed the work in his area. Even so, there were still problems caused by the lack of funding, and it was not until 1892, when financial support was at last obtained from the Reichstag, that the Reichslimeskommission was set up.

Work now proceeded apace, with limited excavation work taking place at each of the main forts, followed by as prompt a publication of the results as was possible. Work at the fort of Unterböbingen, carried out in just a month in September and October 1892, is typical of the pattern followed at many. During the course of this work, the outline of the defences and the layout of the main axes of the fort were established, gate plans were examined, and profiles were cut across the ditches and

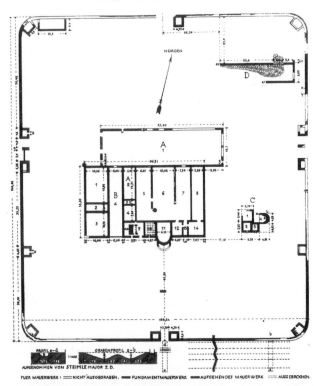

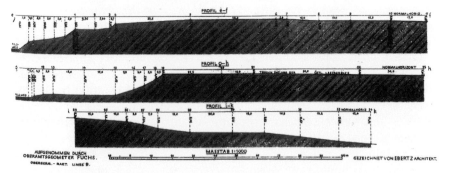

Figure 5 The fort at Unterböbingen, from *Der obergermanische Limes*. This plan was recovered from the site in the course of a single month's work

the fort walls. The defences were examined at several places, and the presence of interval towers was established. The headquarters building at the centre of the fort, measuring 50 by 70 metres, came in for close scrutiny, and its full plan, as well as that of a small bath-building next to it, was recorded. Hypocausts were noted in two of the rooms next to the Chapel of the Standards. Further work within the fort located a portion of a stable or barrack accommodation in its north-east corner, and exploration outside the fort recorded traces of two other buildings lying to its east. The published account gives a description of all the rooms and buildings, a plan of the fort showing what was excavated and what was assumed to exist, and a location plan. In the case of Unterböbingen, a selection of finds, including a fragment of a military diploma, is also described and drawn, though few find-spots within the fort are given in any detail. All this was achieved in just four weeks' excavation.

By 1896, funds for excavation and the necessary survey were again found to be inadequate, and the original hopes of completing the task within a short space of time had continually to be revised; excavations were becoming more costly and extensive than had been at first envisaged. The commission was given funding for four further years' work, but this took little account of the evolving nature of archaeological work: further funding in some cases served only to expose how little was known, and therefore how inadequate some of the earlier answers and the quality of the research had been. By 1901, thirty-four of the frontier forts, less than half of those whose existence was known, had been partially explored by excavation and the results published. By 1903, it had been decided that excavation ought to cease, and that the major responsibility was the publication of the results of this first, large amount of work, a task which fell to Ernst Fabricius, who had been appointed to head the commission in 1898. By 1914 work in the field had actually stopped, and the last of the major series of reports on this section of the Roman frontier eventually appeared in 1937.

This pattern of serious planned research linked to full publication of the results was not followed in all other European countries. In Italy during the course of the earlier part of the nineteenth century, fresh sites were keenly sought and, once found, were exploited for their finds of statues and inscriptions to satisfy the dealers' markets and tempt the purses of *cognoscenti*. One of the sites exploited in this way was Ostia, the port of Rome, which had already by the end of the eighteenth century received the attentions of excavators desirous of finding 'objects of taste'. With the sanction of the pope, excavations there were begun in 1802. The report on this rather haphazard digging touched only on part of the work which had been carried out. Part of the excavators' intention, however, had been not merely to hunt for statues and objects of art, but to plan and record any structures which were uncovered. Although it is clear that the forum baths, the basilica, the Capitolium and the Round Temple were all explored at this time, accounts of only the latter two were included in the resulting publication.

Further excavations took place between 1824 and 1834, but more systematic work was not undertaken until the middle of the century. Even now, the rationale for the work was to supply further treasures for the papal palace, and the excavator, Visconti, had to tread a fine line between a hunt for artifacts which would satisfy his patron, and work which could achieve one of his own main aims – the elucidation through excavation of the history of the site. These excavations came to an end in 1870. All that had been achieved was the examination of buildings at many scattered points within the town, and work had concentrated on those areas which, on initial exploration, had seemed likeliest to bring the best reward. Publication of the results was equally scanty and haphazard, and it was not until early in the 1900s that a more considered policy and strategically planned research initiative were in evidence at Ostia. The foundations for future work had by then been laid by scholars such as Dessau, who in the late nineteenth century had carefully collected and published all the known inscriptions from the site.

Other areas had fared rather better. In Britain, interest in the Romans had peaked as a result of the continuing spectacular finds at Pompeii. Their influence on the artistic repertoire of men such as Adam, whose designs for interiors and exteriors of country houses drew on classical motifs, was immense. Equally affected was Josiah Wedgwood, whose Etruria pottery works established in 1769 in Staffordshire owed its name as well as the inspiration for many of the products themselves to the reawakened interest in Roman and Etruscan antiquities, newly illustrated in publications by William Hamilton and others. In Britain itself, attention had switched to the discovery and description of antiquities of all periods, continuing and developing the tradition established by Camden and various county historians in the sixteenth and seventeenth centuries.

Apart from the sustained interest in those sites and monuments like Hadrian's Wall which were still clearly to be seen, the most obvious and distinctively Roman finds were those of mosaic pavements. The existence of a large Roman mosaic in the churchyard at Woodchester, Gloucestershire, for example, was already known at the end of the seventeenth century. Parts of it were unearthed from time to time in the course of the eighteenth, and detailed drawings made. Its design, showing Orpheus surrounded by a menagerie of beasts, had been established by 1722, but the exploration of the extent of the villa to which it belonged, still one of the largest known in Britain, was only undertaken by Samuel Lysons in the 1790s, when the occasion of the excavation of a vault in the churchyard was exploited to enable a considerable portion of the

Figure 6 Drawing by Lysons of the mosaic at Woodchester. This shows portions of the mosaic, including the elephant, which are now lost

pavement to be laid open. His full-colour drawings of the mosaics and his plans of the rest of the villa, which contained at least ten other mosaics, are still the most complete record which exists of the site. Though recent re-examination of the site and the mosaic has shown that his drawings may not be absolutely accurate – his drawing of the mosaic, for instance, is not exactly as he must have seen it, but rather more a restoration of what he felt ought to have been there – they represent a major step forward in the presentation of solid evidence about sites and discoveries which has laid the groundwork for much refinement between his day and ours. Lysons was an influential figure, and his major publications, of which the lavishly illustrated volume on Woodchester was one, included a series of books called *Reliquiae Britannico-Romanae*, published between 1813 and 1817, which started to record and present the wealth of Roman material in Britain, and included accounts of several of the major known villas in the country and their mosaics, such as those of Bignor, Sussex, and Horkstow, South Humberside.

Excavations were also on occasion undertaken by a society formed for the purpose of exploring a particular site. One of the earliest of these was set up to examine the Roman fort on the bank of the River Danube at Schlögen in Austria, closely followed in the 1840s and 1850s by excavations undertaken by the newly formed Austrian Landesmuseum at Lauriacum, the legionary fortress of Lorch. Publication, which included ground-plans and a description of selection of the finds, followed smartly on the heels of these campaigns of excavation, and may have formed something of a spur for the university of Vienna to concern itself with the major site on its doorstep – 'that Pompeii before the gates of Vienna', Carnuntum. The fact that the plan of the legionary fortress at Carnuntum is known in such detail today is the product of systematic excavation there which began in 1877, and which ran with the support of state and private donations virtually in an unbroken sequence until 1913.

This was only one of many sites uncovered in the same way during the course of the nineteenth century and in its latter part in particular, when many substantial campaigns of excavation at some of the major sites of the Roman world were set in train. Much of this work involved what we would now describe as 'wall-chasing' – the sort of work which would seek to uncover the ground-plans of buildings, but which would not record in too much detail what levels and layers had to be gone through (and removed) in order to reveal the structure itself. Worse still from our point of view today, the technique of following walls and thereby establishing a ground-plan might often mean that they became separated from virtually all of the layers and levels which had built up around them. This effectively destroyed for all time any trace of the archaeological context between walls and other layers which sometimes might have been the clue to their relationship with the remainder of the structure.

A new concept, that of recording Roman and other remains in advance of their destruction by building work or other disturbance, was already starting to gain ground in the course of the nineteenth century. Impetus for certain excavation campaigns was given either by the discovery of a new and previously unsuspected site in the countryside, or by the chance revelation of earlier structures within builders' trenches. This happened, for example, at South Shields at the mouth of the River Tyne in 1875, when the Church Commissioners sold the site of the Roman fort to developers for a new housing estate. Here immediate excavations were undertaken, and a portion of the centre of the fort, containing a considerable number of granaries and its headquarters building, was left free from housing as the 'Roman remains' park. When the growth of the outer suburbs of Newcastle imposed a similar threat on the site of Wallsend fort, at the east end of Hadrian's Wall, in 1883, houses were allowed to cover the entire fort although some recording work was undertaken. Thus urban rescue archaeology had its embryonic beginnings, though many decades had to pass before public and private funding bodies became convinced of the need to support this type of archaeology.

One of the leaders in this field was London, whose Roman origins had already been noted by Sir Christopher Wren while he was engaged in the task of rebuilding part of the city destroyed by the Great Fire in 1666. The expansion of building and sewerage systems in London during the course of the middle years of the nineteenth century brought a great number of new Roman finds to light, and these were watched and recorded to the best of his ability by a city pharmacist, Charles Roach Smith. By visiting builders' sites in progress, Smith was able to record where the major finds had been made, and started to form a collection of artifacts of many different dates from the city.

His insistent pressure on the city authorities that they should do something about the destruction of the earlier levels of London fell initially on deaf ears, but eventually led them to form a small museum at the Guildhall. Roach Smith meanwhile had opened his own museum and published a catalogue of his collection. By 1854, ill-health forced him to leave London and to retire, and he sold his material to the British Museum. He had done enough, however, to ensure that there was great interest in the Roman past in the city, and when in 1869 a new mosaic was revealed in Queen Victoria Street, people came out to see it in their thousands, and the Lord Mayor attempted to make provision for lifting it and preserving it in the museum. Destruction continued, however, and the best efforts of interested observers and antiquaries could not keep pace with the amount of building work which was under way. Despite one or two major excavations with fine results, such as that near the Tower of London on the bastion of the Roman wall in Camomile Street, all that could realistically be achieved within the heavily built-up area of central London was the recording of fragmentary remains which might one day contribute to a more fruitful large-scale study of the Roman city. Even so, the work was able to pinpoint certain areas, e.g. that of the basilica and forum, which would be worth pursuing in the future, should occasion arise. The magnitude of the task in a site such as London, where the Roman strata are buried anything up to four metres deep beneath the detritus and remains of other buildings of other periods, meant that large-scale work of the sort carried out, for example, at Silchester, where the whole of the town plan was examined, was impossible.

The spectacle of thousands of the inhabitants of the city of London visiting the site of the Queen Victoria Street mosaic in 1869 shows the

Figure 7 Visitors to the excavations at the Mansion House, London, in 1869

extent to which Roman archaeology had by then, as it were, arrived on people's doorsteps. Until the early nineteenth century, the pursuit of archaeology had been carried out by the well-to-do in far off lands. The tradition of touring ancient sites primarily to assist in the wider education of a nobleman or gentleman was firmly established in the eighteenth century. The nineteenth, with greater opportunities for travel in many places of the world, saw an increase in the numbers of people able and willing to visit archaeological sites. For much of the century, this was still restricted to those who had the considerable means necessary to enable them to travel.

Italy was still one of the primary targets, and sites such as Pompeii and Ostia were favourites among those who still performed the Grand Tour. The Near East, however, was a more exotic area for exploration, and sites such as Palmyra, Baalbek, and Petra, all of which had been visited and described by several Europeans during the course of the eighteenth century, had considerable numbers of new visitors in the nineteenth, both tourists and scholars. One of the most colourful of the tourists was Lady Hester Stanhope, once the society hostess of the British Prime Minister William Pitt, who spent much of her annuity of £1,500 per annum which she received from his will in travelling throughout the eastern Mediterranean area. With a large retinue of hangers-on and servants, she decided in 1813 to visit Palmyra, and there are lively accounts of her arrival there, her reception by the Syrian chiefs who occupied the site, and of her stay. It was the scholars, however, rather than such colourful characters as these, who provided the more lasting accounts of the sites, and many of them sketched or drew portions of the remains which, supplemented by their accounts of what they saw, have proved useful records of buildings which are now more ruined than they were then. There were still new sites awaiting discovery: the first western traveller to arrive at Jerash in 1806 was able to remark in considerable surprise that its ruins might be compared to those of Palmyra or Baalbek. Exploration in this area was fostered by the newly formed Palestine Association, whose functions and interests were taken over by the Royal Geographical Society in 1834.

Serious study of the remains of these cities of the eastern Mediterranean was not undertaken until the later decades of the century – Jerash under the auspices of the Palestine Exploration Fund and their own archaeologist and surveyor in 1875. At Palmyra and Baalbek, the initiative for close study came from a visit by the German Kaiser Wilhelm II in 1898. He was so impressed by the site of Baalbek after the briefest of visits that under his orders the Prussian Ministry of Culture commissioned and paid for a survey of the remains between 1900 and 1902. This survey, which involved the planning of the structures of the temples as they stood, the recording of all extraneous buildings removed from them during the course of the excavation, and the use of photogrammetric techniques to draw and record all the wall-surfaces, is a pioneer of its kind. Baalbek having been dealt with, a similar study was started at Palmyra; this lasted from 1902 to 1917.

Less exotic places, too, began to receive attention. Another of the major projects undertaken by Wilhelm II was the excavation of the complete fort on the German *limes* at the Saalburg in the 1880s and 1890s, which led eventually to the rebuilding of the walls and some of the internal buildings between 1898 and 1907. At the same time, a museum was established there, as had also happened a little earlier at Chesters, on Hadrian's Wall – a clear sign that there was a need to feed the interest of a growing number of visitors who sought information and enlightenment about the past. Then as now, the appeal of archaeology began to enliven public interest and awareness. This might mean the prospect of attracting a newly mobile populace to see for themselves what the Roman period had to offer, and to establish display collections or sites where museums could be set up to cater especially for the tourist. Guide-books started to appear – indeed the first editions of Collingwood Bruce's *Handbook to the Roman Wall* published in 1856 had been intended as a guide to the

Figure 8 The reconstructed headquarters building at the Saalburg, Bad Homburg, Germany

remains of Hadrian's Wall for the visitor, and associated surveys and maps also assisted tourists to make the most of their trip. The excavators at Silchester in the 1890s had to cope with flocks of visitors on Sundays, but this all helped to keep the work in the public eye and to justify the appeal to the public for funds for further work.

The nineteenth century had seen a great deal uncovered, but its excavators had by and large lacked the skill or the understanding for a full interpretation of what was found. A wider vision of the potential returns from archaeological work was necessary, both in terms of the study of finds excavated from Roman and other sites, and in terms of understanding better the processes of deposition of sequences of archaeological soils and layers. Where substantial stone Roman buildings still stood, there was perhaps little impetus for this sort of research: what was important there was to record the remains, relate any building inscriptions discovered to the standing structures (thus dating them), and ensure that they were completely exposed in all their glory. In areas such as Britain, however, where there was a scarcity of major standing Roman buildings, the position was rather different. Here, although the foundation plan of much of a Roman city such as Silchester could be exposed in a campaign of excavation, there were many sites where the excavated remains were far more fragmentary, where the structures uncovered did not seem always to have been of stone, and where there was no readily available dating evidence apart from a few scraps of fairly undistinguished pottery or other artifacts. Further progress in extracting the archaeological story from the ground required a more systematic approach to this type of excavated material. One man, towards the latter part of the nineteenth century, had begun to lay the foundations for this through his work in southern England. He was Augustus Henry Lane Fox, later to take the name Pitt-Rivers.

3

The twentieth century:
changes in technique and emphasis

Pitt-Rivers, born in 1827, received a military training and saw active service at home and abroad with the Grenadier Guards, most actively in the Crimean War in the 1850s. His interests, however, allied to his military service, encouraged him to study the effectiveness of weaponry, and he was responsible for a study of the theory and practice of musketry. This was of practical use for the British Army's development, as well as being of considerable theoretical use to Pitt-Rivers himself, since it enabled him to study the development of a particular form of artifact – the rifle – and to begin to formulate certain fundamental principles which were later to help him in his studies of the typology of various kinds of archaeological material.

During the course of the 1850s and 1860s, Pitt-Rivers's interests in the study of the past were aroused and he fell in with a group of influential men much stimulated by the Darwinian theories of natural selection then current. Pitt-Rivers's interest in excavated material from Ireland, where he had been stationed for part of his military career, coupled with these theories, encouraged him to formulate his own views and to apply them to developments in the design of archaeological artifacts, as well as providing the impetus to start his own collection of material for study. His involvement in archaeological work led to his semi-retirement (on half-pay) from the army in 1867, and he devoted part of his new-found leisure to the study of excavations then current on some of the prehistoric barrow sites of Yorkshire being undertaken by Canon Greenwell. From Greenwell, he began to understand the importance not only of the excavated material itself, but of the context and its relationship to the structures from which it came, in forming an overall view of what information could be imparted by its study.

His first formal excavations took place at the hill-fort of Cissbury Ring in southern England; technically these were not a great success, but they perhaps provided material which he was able to use in the formation of a type-series of flint artifacts. This was followed by further work on barrow sites in Wessex, and by improvements both in the techniques of excavating such structures and in the methods of recording the work which had been done. For example, his methods now included careful

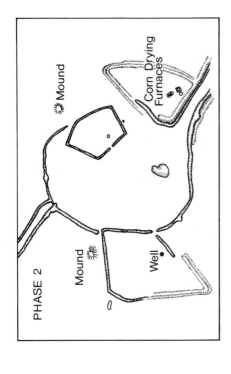

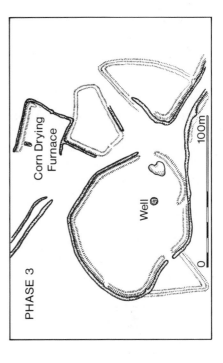

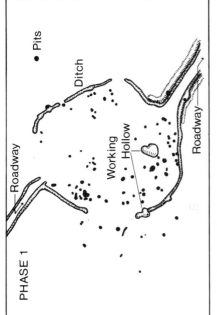

Figure 9 Pitt-Rivers's work at Woodcuts Roman farmstead. From Pitt-Rivers's original (unphased) plans, it was possible for C.F.C. Hawkes to reinterpret these three main phases of use of site: Phase 1, first to mid second century; Phase 2, mid second to early fourth century; Phase 3, early fourth century to about AD370

recording on section drawings of the layers uncovered and cut through. His excavation work received even greater impetus when, in 1880, he inherited the major estate left to him by Lord Rivers at Cranborne Chase. Not only did this translate him suddenly into a substantial and wealthy landowner and force him under the terms of the bequest to change his name (it had been Lane Fox) to Pitt-Rivers, but it also made him the owner of a substantial portion of southern England which was rich in prehistoric and Roman remains.

For the study of Roman archaeology, it is perhaps the excavations at the native-type but Roman period sites at Woodcuts and at Rotherley on the Cranborne Estate which are his most significant contribution. Until the middle years of the 1880s, Pitt-Rivers had concentrated largely on prehistoric remains – barrow burials and hill-forts – mainly in an effort to gain more material for his typological collections of flints and other artifacts. These Iron Age or Romano-British village sites, however, were less obvious targets for excavation work to judge from their surface remains. When examined, they produced only a series of less than distinct traces of disturbances in the chalk subsoil, which when planned and meticulously recorded were interpreted as drains (ditches) and pits. A number of hypocausted structures were also located, and the sites as a whole were interpreted as native villages in Roman style. The significance of this work was not fully revealed, however, until about sixty years later, when the published material, plans and sections from the Cranborne Chase volumes, was reassessed in the light of other more recent excavations at the nearby site of Little Woodbury, and the 'villages' of Pitt-Rivers reinterpreted as farmsteads of pre- or early Roman type. His work, however, and more importantly his careful recording and publication, had formed the basis for improved understanding of the nature of the excavated sites at a later stage and in the light of better data from elsewhere. This was an important principle.

Pitt-Rivers died in 1900, and the example he had shown in his methods of approach to the archaeological evidence was not immediately followed; it was not, perhaps, until the 1930s that some of the techniques he had pioneered would be more fully applied. In general, by the early years of the twentieth century enthusiasm for archaeological work had grown apace in many parts of the Roman world. Excavation and restoration of the remains of the Roman city had begun under French direction at Timgad (Thamugadi) in Algeria in 1881, and this was the African centre of a network of archaeological exploration which expanded to include work at a number of other major sites. Although many such sites were examined in part, more comprehensive campaigns of excavation and research took place in the early years of the twentieth century at Timgad, Cuicul, Lepcis Magna, and Sabratha.

Whilst there was a self-imposed moratorium on new excavation work on the Roman frontiers in Germany, pending the publication of the results of earlier work by the Reichslimeskommission, other areas had no such barriers to expansion. Excavations continued at Carnuntum in Austria, resulting by 1911 in the recovery of virtually the complete plan of the Roman legionary fortress. Similarly, in Switzerland, a local society aimed at the excavation and display of the legionary fortress of Vindonissa was established in 1897. Annual excavations took place, and this led not only to the establishment (in 1912) of a major museum collection, but to the piecemeal exploration of parts of the site which led eventually to the formulation of a near-complete plan. In Britain, excavations took place at Corbridge, near Hadrian's Wall, between 1906 and 1914, in a campaign which was to establish much of the complex plan of the central portion of this Roman site. Fuller understanding of the remains had, however, to await further, more detailed work some years later, but for much of the site, the excavation in the early decades of this century remains to this day the only record. Much the same is true also of the Roman town of Caerwent in Wales, excavated between 1899 and 1913.

This was the period of the establishment by excavation of ground-plans of many of the more obvious buildings of these and many other major Roman sites. Research was orientated along these lines for many years. The drawback, however, which made this kind of research rather less satisfactory than it seemed at first sight, was the fact that the production of these ground-plans alone made little or no distinction between the various phases or periods of building represented. To assume that the plan recovered by a necessarily unselective excavation of the ground-plan of a fortress, fort, or town was typical of several sites, especially when the plan produced contained a considerable amalgam of buildings of various dates and periods, was dangerous. For some sites – Pompeii, Herculaneum, Timgad, or the French site of Vaison-la-Romaine which was also under excavation at this period – the approach would bear considerable fruit. For other sites, like Corbridge, where the remains themselves were not so readily identifiable and where the excavations could only proceed piecemeal, by uncovering and then reburying new areas year by year, there were and still are considerable problems of interpretation.

The early years of the century were also a formative period for studies of pottery and other artifacts, in particular the ubiquitous Roman pottery known as *terra sigillata* (Samian ware). The classification of its several common forms, in both plain and decorated wares, the quantification and publication of accounts or drawings of pottery from a number of (mainly military) sites from all parts of the empire, and the identification of the various fabrics and factories in southern and central Gaul which were its main production centres, all helped to build up the use to which this material could be put in determining the periods at which various standard forms or styles of decoration were common. Much of this kind of dating might be felt to rely unacceptably on a tenuous relationship between the finds from a site and the historically attested presence there of a particular unit of troops. Thus considerable argument raged about the date of the Roman advance into and first abandonment of Scotland as part of the conquests of Agricola, based on conflicting interpretations of the Samian found at a range of Scottish sites and on the dating not only of those sites, but of other places in Britain and abroad where similar material was found. There were those who virtually despaired of using Samian as a reliable dating tool at all, and who found that the series of historical theories built upon the foundation of a few sherds of pottery here or there might lead to ultimately unsatisfactory conclusions.

One of the areas, however, where the results from pottery studies and archaeological work were to bear a good deal of fruit in the period between the world wars, following considerable advances made before the outbreak of the First World War, was the northern frontier of Britain. Work carried out by the Cumberland Excavation Committee at the western end of Hadrian's Wall was matched by the enthusiasm of the North of England Excavation Committee in Northumberland at the eastern end. A determined assault was made on establishing the structural sequence of the wall and its associated forts and other features. This began at Greatchesters fort, but gained greatest impetus from the examination of the fort of Birdoswald and the area around it.

Here, judicious excavation of limited areas examined the relationship between the fort and Hadrian's Wall, here first built of turf and only later completed in stone, and then succeeded in fitting the vallum, the earthwork system of ditch and banks which follows the line of Hadrian's Wall across the country, into its correct sequence within the system. The work revealed that Hadrian's Wall had been first planned without forts, and that the decision to add them to the frontier was a relatively rapid one, taken before much of the building work on the wall itself had been completed. Since the vallum was seen to deviate round several of the forts, it was clear that this was the next element in the system to be completed (thus destroying any lingering thoughts that the vallum may have been an earlier barrier superseded by the wall itself), and this, too, was in one or two cases overlain by further forts added to the wall-line. The complex sequence of developments which was revealed, mainly by means of small-scale examination of elements of the Hadrianic frontier system, was a triumph for the methodology of approach which saw brilliant deductive logic applied to the problems of the wall and its features on a large scale.

During the middle years of the twentieth century, there was a continuing refinement of techniques of excavation for sites of all periods. In this, Roman sites do not necessarily furnish the best examples of the

Figure 10 Aerial view of Birdoswald Roman fort. The site of the excavations in the 1920s and 1930s was largely in the area between the fort and the edge of the escarpment to its south

different methods which were commonly applied. However, a number of examples, selected from Britain alone, may serve to show the range of approaches to the problems and methods of excavation adopted by different and highly influential people.

Major excavations begun under the direction of Sir J.P. Bushe-Fox at the site of Richborough in the 1920s and 1930s made use of large-scale open areas of excavation, with the clearance, in certain cases, of massive amounts of deposited material from occupation or destruction layers within the fort or its ditches. By contrast, excavations by Sir Mortimer Wheeler at sites such as Maiden Castle, Verulamium, or the Roman temple at Lydney began, at least, by making use of the grid method which he favoured. According to this, the area under excavation was split up into regular squares leaving narrow unexcavated baulks between the areas under initial examination, which could be removed later if required, but which for the time being contained a permanent record of the layers

35

Figure 11 Richborough under excavation in 1926. Note the depth of layers which have been cut through in order to follow the walls of this building

which had been cut through as part of the work. Elsewhere, as at the excavation of the Roman fort of Fendoch in Scotland in the later 1930s, Sir Ian Richmond made use of an even more selective method: by exploring portions of the site with diagonal trenches, set at 45 degrees to the Roman building line, the traces of Roman timber buildings whose beam-trenches or post-holes were cut into the subsoil could be intercepted and identified quite rapidly. With a minimum of effort, and from limited numbers of trenches, deductions could be made as to the overall plan of the site under examination without having to go to the considerable expense of excavating the whole site.

These three methods of excavation of different Roman sites merit a little further examination. Despite the fact that the sites were excavated in the 1920s and 1930s, they can serve as object lessons for the problems of approach and interpretation which face archaeologists specializing in any period, but the fact that all the sites have some Roman element makes these different techniques interesting for an assessment of the historical development of the archaeological examination of Roman sites.

Richborough was a very complex site, with several different layers of superimposed strata containing evidence for nearly four centuries of occupation. Methods and techniques of area excavation carried out in the 1920s, mainly with labour provided by local workmen under relatively scant supervision, meant that much of the detail of ephemeral (probably timber) structures in some of the uppermost layers of the site must have gone unrecorded; it was only on reaching either substantial stone buildings in the upper layers or the cleaner subsoil that a complete plan of structures, beam-slots and post-holes could be recognized. The subsoil in particular revealed a complex foundation layout of timber buildings which had occupied the site. Fragmentary masonry buildings were also encountered at various points and at several different levels within the excavation, but these were rarely comprehensive enough to afford a picture of the full layout at any particular phase of the Roman use of the site. If an excavator were to be carrying out this work today, he ought not to be content with his results unless his examination of the site revealed a full sequence of phase-plans covering the whole of the interior: this would include the careful analysis of changes in the soils which could reveal the positions of timber buildings and building platforms for all phases of the site's use, not just the bottom-most. Some more determined attempts were made in the latter years of excavation at the site to remedy this omission, but the comprehensive nature of the excavation and the lack of techniques which could adequately deal with the full complexities of such a site have meant that our understanding of the full history and development of this important port, town, and defended base is necessarily incomplete.

Sir Mortimer Wheeler, a highly influential figure in British archaeology between the wars, was a forthright critic of both his own archaeological work and many other people's. More than anyone else, he brought order and method to the science of archaeological excavation and had some very harsh words to say about those who he considered did not match up to his high standards. His own view of his excavations at the late Iron Age hill-fort of Maiden Castle in southern England is revealing. He records that in 1935 he excavated part of one of the entrances to the hill-fort by trenching (that is, digging a number of irregularly placed and separate trenches), and was appalled at the complexity of the record this method produced. In the succeeding year, by excavating another of the entrances by means of a regular grid of square trenches, excavation and recording work were far easier. Thus, the principle of an orderly approach to the task of excavation was vindicated, and the implantation of a methodical system would serve to set the whole task on a sound footing.

Anyone who starts out to excavate a site by laying out a grid of trenches has, however, to be prepared eventually to convert this grid where necessary into an open area excavation, and this is what Wheeler did, more often than not. The grid method is suitable for relatively simple structures, but it produces its own problems when, as seems often to be the case, what appears in one excavated square is completely different from what appears in the one next to it. In addition, the difficulty of being certain that walls, ditches, pits, or other features which appear in one trench are in fact related to or the same as those in the one nextdoor, and the problems of consistency of description of these remains (when responsibility for recording the two areas falls to two separate individuals) make the grid system less helpful in practice. As an attempt to impose some form of disciplined approach to a site, and particularly a Roman site where the remains may well bear some relationship to a grid of trenches laid out over it, this method of excavation made a great deal of sense, and was widely adopted. Not everyone was as successful as Wheeler in transcending the limitations of the approach to produce similar results from different sites to which he was as often as not able to give a flamboyant and historically attractive interpretation.

Richmond's approach to excavation, albeit brilliant in conception, could also cause problems through its very selectivity. It was most useful on single-period sites, such as the Roman military sites of Fendoch or Inchtuthil, and it relied in heavy measure on the quintessential regularity of layout of such military installations. Much of the recorded plan of a site like Fendoch, now recognized as a key type-site as far as fort layout is concerned, is in fact based on a limited but strategic number of keyhole trenches to check particular alignments or identify the limits of key buildings. It is therefore in large measure a restored plan, whose reliability depends both on the extent to which Roman military engineers and planners did in fact maintain regular layouts, and on the brilliance of interpretation of a number of disjointed post-holes or beam-trenches which assigns them to specific types of building always expected to turn up within a Roman fort of this or that era.

In a sense, this excavation method employs a dangerously circular argument: it assumes that elements of a certain layout will be encountered, and is geared up to finding and identifying them. Provided the evidence can be interpreted as fitting into some form of the standard pattern (largely established by the use of similar methods elsewhere), the whole of the site plan can be restored by a combination of analogy, deduction, and guesswork. Thus, by examining perhaps as little as a tenth of the site, spectacularly complete results, not necessarily false in outline,

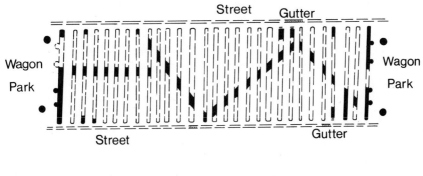

= = = Conjectured Areas

Street   Gutter

Wagon

Park

Wagon

Park

Street   Gutter

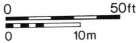

0   50ft

0   10m

Figure 12 Plan of one of the granaries at Inchtuthil legionary fortress. The areas actually excavated are shown in solid black; this plan shows how much can be conjectured from a series of well–placed trenches across a regular building

but possibly self-perpetuating, are produced. Excavations of Roman military installations in many parts of the Roman world, in which a large area is examined in detail, have now begun to show how consistently irregular these sites actually are: thus the archaeologist of today must begin to look carefully at the basis of deductions about 'standard layouts' made by this method of recording. It is a positive bonus, however, that this minimal approach to the examination of Roman military installations has in fact left the greater part of most of them untouched, and still awaiting examination.

This concentration on work in Britain during the inter-war period is not to claim that the work here was any more important than that elsewhere. Considerable work was taking place in Italy at the time, and this included the examination and restoration of major monuments within the city of Rome such as the Mausoleum of Augustus and the Ara Pacis. At Ostia, excavations were proceeding, slowly at first, but with gathering momentum towards the end of the period, with greater emphasis being given to the exploration of the origins and development of the town than merely to the clearance of further areas of buildings. Elsewhere in Europe, although efforts on the German frontier zones were still mainly directed towards publication of excavations already undertaken, some work was done, for example the exploration of the double legionary fortress of Vetera, near Xanten. In southern Germany, the excavation was undertaken of the late Roman 'burgus' site of the Bürgle by one of the most proficient excavators of the day, Gerald Bersu. Other major work was taking place in France, Switzerland, and other European countries on a scale unparalleled before. Further afield, a joint team of excavators, mainly American, began to tackle the site of Dura Europos, a focal contact point between the Romans and the Persian empire to the east.

The inter-war period saw great advances in the historical conclusions addressed by the examination of archaeological sites. Perhaps not surprisingly, too, there was something of a concentration on the distinctive 'national' identity of individual Roman provinces: studies with titles such as 'Belgium in the Roman Period', 'The Earliest History of the Netherlands', 'Roman Britain', and 'Switzerland in Roman Times' are typical of this time. They all show how extensive was the range of material available for study, how specialized and compartmentalized the study of individual Roman areas (not necessarily even subdivided by 'provinces') needed to be, and how urgent the search for individual historical and chronological frameworks for excavated sites within regional areas was becoming. What mattered greatly was the search for definable historical events which could be tied into the archaeological data, thus giving a reliable series of date-horizons within which the archaeological periods could be fitted.

One of the best examples of this was once again on the northern British frontier of Hadrian's Wall. Analysis of excavated material from a variety of sites, and excavation data from new campaigns of digging, suggested that the history of the wall could be broken down into four main periods. The first was represented by the construction of the wall and its associated structures, begun in the early 120s and completed towards the end of that decade. The second phase, known as period Ib, represented reoccupation of Hadrian's Wall in the middle years of the second century after the Romans had pushed forward to the Antonine Wall between the Forth and the Clyde from 139 to the late 150s. The end of wall period I was set unhesitatingly in the year 197, when Clodius Albinus removed part of the garrison of Britain to fight in Gaul. There are inscriptions from the wall area which suggest that some reconstruction of forts was necessary, and damage is attested in the archaeological record in the later second century at four of the wall-sites. This damage and consequent reconstruction was pegged to the historically known date of 197 when it was claimed the wall was overrun by tribesmen from the north and widespread damage was caused. This second period on the wall came to an end in 296; two inscriptions from wall-forts suggest that there was some rebuilding after this date, again pegged to a historically known situation, when Roman rule was re-established over Britain after the episode of usurpation by Carausius and Allectus. The reimposition of Roman order meant a new beginning on the northern frontier. The end of the third period came in 367 when, according to the historian Ammianus Marcellinus, there was a barbarian conspiracy which was able to launch a successful attack on the province. Wall period IV, the supposed restoration of the northern frontier after this date, was short-lived, and is not attested by any inscription recording rebuilding.

This framework, or model, for the historical interpretation of the wall and its remains served its purpose for much of the middle decades of the century. Although the product of many separate observations and studies of material from the area, it served to relate sites to each other, and it gave a framework into which all sites examined could be expected to fit. Thus, the building of this sort of model on a large scale is both a help and a hindrance: it helps to clarify and classify the large body of material on which the historical model is based in the first place, and it forms a focus for further research and consideration of the problems. However, it can act as a considerable barrier to progress, in that it may force new data to be sculpted to fit existing theories when in fact it should be recognized as forming a conflict with them, requiring them to be revised. In addition, the model put forward for Hadrian's Wall as a whole begs a number of fundamental questions which need to be clarified: why should all destruction on the wall be attributed to enemy action concentrated on one particular event or date? What justification is there for linking the 'destructions' of the wall with this or that political event elsewhere? Is it reasonable to assume that a structure eighty Roman miles in length had precisely the same history in the Roman period from end to end? The inherent neatness of some of the answers should begin to rouse suspicions, though the force of most of the evidence cannot be denied, and whatever historical explanation is advanced, this needs to be recognized and given full value.

It is precisely this form of hypothesis, evaluation of the evidence, and testing against new and improved data that is the stuff of archaeological research. As well as providing an opportunity for this essential work of classifying and organizing the results from excavation work, the years before the outbreak of the Second World War saw archaeological practice advance into new fields, still relatively untried. Survey was a primary objective, and the German work on the sites of Palmyra and Baalbek in the early years of the century was followed by other pioneering work, for example by Brünnow and von Domaszewski on the largely Roman military remains in the desert areas of the Near East. Surveying was carried out from the air by Poidébard and Mouterde in similar areas.

Aerial photography in fact was beginning to come into its own as a major tool for archaeologists in the 1920s and 1930s, following the recognition of cropmarks from the air on some aerial views of Stonehenge taken in 1921. More use was to be made of the RAF vertical cover of the country in succeeding years, particularly with regard to the identification of earthwork sites and 'native' settlements in some of the upland areas. A remarkable series of earthworks and cropmarks was revealed in the low-lying Fenlands of Britain. The extent to which aerial photography was a new skill which could capture the imagination is shown by the fact that one aerial shot taken in 1928, showing the town of Caistor-by-Norwich with buildings and street-grids clearly visible, was sufficient impetus to launch a relatively hastily arranged programme of excavation between 1929 and 1935 at the site by a research committee set up for the purpose. Publication of many of the results, however, had for a variety of reasons to wait until 1971.

This highlights another of the growing problems of archaeology, and one which is with us still: there is an overriding obligation to present the results of excavation in a form in which others can see what has been done, including making readily available a sufficient body of evidence to enable the reader to check the conclusions reached by the excavator. Some early publications, including that of the excavations at Richborough, and those of Wheeler and Richmond, were prompt and exemplary in their clarity and presentation. Other excavators clearly found the publication of their results an increasing burden, particularly where the excavations had produced considerable amounts of pottery or other material for study, and where the necessary synthesis entailed a greater proportion of time spent on this aspect of archaeological work.

Interpretation, too, was all important. Archaeology was becoming ever more public, with the increasing upsurge of interest shown in the growth of museums and excavations funded by public subscription and support. Wheeler himself was one of the greatest showmen, more fully exploited after the advent of television, but he was able to excavate the amphitheatre of the legionary fortress of Caerleon in 1926–8 with funding support from the *Daily Mail*. As an interpreter of his excavations, and helping to tell a good story based upon the remains, he was perhaps unrivalled: at Maiden Castle this was assisted by the discovery of the gruesome remains of a body with a Roman ballista-bolt embedded in its spine. The bolt had entered from the front, and provided dramatic evidence of the 'last stand' at Maiden Castle on the part of the Iron Age population faced by the Roman invasion force sweeping down through southern Britain in AD43. Perhaps the more dramatic historical interpretation of a large-scale site came in Wheeler's excavations and survey work at Stanwick, the large late Iron Age fortification in northern England. The growth and development of the complex series of fortifications was linked with the historically attested events surrounding the Roman advance into this area of Britain in the AD70s. It is only in very recent years that this historical model has been seriously challenged by new data and new interpretations.

At all events, this form of presentation of the evidence, with its wide appeal, did much to set archaeology on the map as a serious subject for study, certainly in Britain in this inter-war period. Despite the growth in public interest, the formation of local archaeological societies, and the existence of major campaigns of excavation work, it was still the preserve of very few professional people, and it was certainly relatively poorly funded. Implications for the necessary growth in funding to take both excavation and publication work into account had not yet been grasped, and, apart perhaps from within Germany, there was no communal self-discipline which would ensure that results from work carried out so far would be processed before further strides forward would be taken. In many places – Ostia, Rome, Pompeii as well as other European sites – publication was beginning seriously to lag behind excavation work. Much had been achieved, but the outbreak of the war put a brake on most of the work in progress.

The onset of the war interrupted a great deal of archaeological work, but also highlighted some of the potential which had been latent for a long time. The principle had already begun to be established that sites under threat of destruction or disturbance in the normal course of events – new building or quarrying, for example – should be excavated in advance. This was difficult to put into practice effectively during wartime in Britain, but there were one or two Roman sites excavated on this basis during the period, some as a result of work carried out in rural areas on the formation of new aerodromes, others in areas of former pasture converted hastily to arable to grow much needed crops. The summaries devoted to the previous year's archaeological work in Britain published annually in the *Journal of Roman Studies* show that a limited amount of excavation work was still possible, even within the necessarily straitened circumstances.

These brief summaries of work undertaken, however, serve to show just how crippling to positive research the onset of war was. In the account of work done in 1939, just before the war began, more than sixty excavations and other items of news or discoveries were reported: in 1940, there were only fourteen, and for the next four years the total of excavations (rather than snippets of survey work) reported on was in no case more than ten per annum. By 1945, however, work had begun to burgeon again, and the task of tackling archaeologically rich deposits in war-damaged areas of some of the major Roman settlements, such as Canterbury, Chester, Lincoln, Exeter, and Southwark, was already beginning.

Work did not cease everywhere as a result of the hostilities. In Italy, a considerable amount of research excavation continued apace. In Rome, research on the Domus Augusta and on the Golden House of Nero was under way, and there had been significant discoveries near the Colosseum, with the finding of the *ludus exercitatoria* – one of the known gladiatorial training schools – nearby. Ostia, too, had seen major excavation work, with a new portion of the town exposed for the first time between the *decumanus maximus* and the river. Work was progressing on other sites, including Aquileia, Pompeii, and Herculaneum, the last at a much slower pace than before because of the extreme difficulties of excavation at such a deeply buried site under the present-day village.

Elsewhere, however, the opportunity afforded by the redevelopment of bomb-damaged areas of historic cities provided the opportunity for positive action. In Britain, this had already begun before the end of the war, in 1943–4, with the formation of a new body, the Council for British Archaeology, whose express aim was to take full advantage of the opportunities afforded, then as never before, by the dereliction of considerable areas of the inner cities. London itself was a prime target, and in 1945 a committee was set up to oversee excavation of the damaged areas, and a director for the work appointed. Funding, however, was always a problem, and the realities of the situation demanded that the work was very selective. Large-scale excavations within the city were not possible. Fifteen years' work were in fact carried out in the city by this committee, its high point perhaps in 1954 with the discovery of the Temple of Mithras, which was accompanied by a great deal of public interest and support. But the relatively small scale of what was practicable, coupled with the considerable difficulties, hitherto largely outside most people's experience, of excavation in a deeply stratified urban context, meant that the results were perhaps not as satisfying as might have been expected.

Urban archaeology was a new field which archaeologists from many nations had to begin to learn. In Germany, perhaps not surprisingly, there were priorities other than archaeology in the immediate post-war period, and it was not until the later 1950s or the 1960s, by then too late for the immediate rebuilding, that campaigns of excavation began to take place in major Roman centres like Köln and Mainz. By this time, too, funding from research institutes, museums, and government could be brought to bear on some of the more important sites, such as the analysis of some of the more important areas of Roman Trier, the exploration of the legionary fortress at Mainz, and the complete examination of the fort site of Künzing (Quintana) in Bavaria. These were only a few of the sites tackled within the period. Even so, the occasional disaster could still happen: the site of the substantial Roman villa at Wittlich, near Trier, partially excavated and protected from the worst effects of damage during the building of the *Autobahn* in 1939–40, was sold after the war, and in 1958 planted with trees. A few years later, the motorway was shifted, and the piers of a new bridge carrying it across the River Lieser smashed straight through the south wing, the best preserved portion, of the villa.

The scale of building, reconstruction, expansion, and development in the post-war period has made this kind of unwitting damage to archaeological remains a continual possibility. Whereas much of the

Figure 13 The statues of Mercury (right) and Bacchus (above) from the excavation of the Temple of Mithras, London, in 1954 (Museum of London)

archaeological work on Roman sites in Britain immediately after the war was funded by a variety of bodies – national and local museums, universities, local groups – it soon became clear that a most important contribution would have to be made from national funds if adequate response was to be made to the requirement for examination of archaeological sites in advance of development. The number of excavated sites in Britain supported by government funding grew apace, and the same was undoubtedly true in many other countries. The reason for that funding was the scale of 'rescue' resources required to safeguard and record elements of the national heritage which would otherwise have been irretrievably lost.

It would be possible, though perhaps invidious, to attempt to list the excavated sites and the major achievements in Roman archaeology in the last forty or so years. Inevitably, any such selection would be a thoroughly personal choice, and, for archaeologists at least, rather similar to choosing the best eight gramophone records to take to the desert island. The choice is vast, and one could base one's selection on many different criteria: for instance, spectacular results, as at the late Roman villa of Piazza Armerina; the significance of the archaeological contribution to historical studies, as at Masada in Israel; technical excellence of recording and observation of highly complex structures, as at Wroxeter in England; or the rarity of surviving remains, such as those of timber forts preserved in waterlogged conditions at Valkenburg in Holland.

Work in the last forty years has brought a vast bulk of evidence about the Roman past to light. Some of it is the product of planned research excavation, with specified objectives, on land or under water. Some comes from reconnaissance from the air or through other survey techniques, aimed at increasing the scope of knowledge of Roman settlement patterns in given areas. Other discoveries are the result of set-piece excavation for the display of a site to visitors, to increase its educational potential or to promote tourism; yet others are purely chance finds thrown up unexpectedly during the course of building operations, or the product of intensive salvage work in the teeth of demolition or construction projects of all kinds. Perhaps less frequently, in view of the increasing costs of excavation and the need to concentrate efforts and resources where they are most needed, sites are excavated for the excitement of discovery, or to form a basis for training in the techniques of excavation.

Whatever the framework within which new discoveries are made, however, modern archaeology is a profession with a growing professionalism, aimed at achieving the maximum of useful information from the exercise of studying the remains of the past. In order to do so, new techniques and methods of retrieving information are continually being applied and refined. Most of these spring ultimately from the principles of

Figure 14 Valkenburg fort, Holland, under excavation. The remains of the commandant's wooden house the earliest fort were exceptionally well-preserved

excavation and stratification which guided archaeologists of the past, though modern work has revealed much that is new. The bulk of the remainder of this book is a brief attempt to show how archaeologists of today look at some of their material, and the ways, some of them quite novel, in which different pictures of the past can be formed from careful study of all the information which is locked in the ground. Not only can this be achieved from the examination of unexpected types of evidence, but it can also reveal some surprising and rewarding results.

4

Archaeology and history

Archaeological evidence has a directness in its link with the past. The study of the remains of a Roman villa together with evidence for the land-use of the surrounding area can lead to an assessment of the style and nature of life in the Roman countryside. Conclusions about the environment, the climate, farming practices, and basic farm economics can be drawn on the basis of solid, measurable evidence. Given the right conditions for the survival of remains, the site can reveal what crops were grown, indicate the patterns of rearing and husbandry of stock, and give a measure of the relative wealth of the owner by the scale of the farm buildings, their state of repair, the number of associated smaller farmsteads or 'tied cottages' which may lie in its neighbourhood, and the kinds of luxury or other artifacts found there.

However, because we are dealing with a period where much of the sequence of historical events can be followed from the eye-witness or near-contemporary accounts of Roman writers or other sources, there is an understandable temptation to link archaeological evidence from Roman sites into the more general framework of Roman history. On occasion, in the past, this has seemed an easy link, in which an archaeologist might interpret the remains of his site either by assigning them a general date by association with certain 'datable' material, or by identifying certain specific finds as evidence of a known historical episode. In studying the coins and pottery from each site, the archaeologist is always trying to achieve the former. The latter – the direct link with historical events – is far harder to achieve with certainty. When Wheeler dug at Maiden Castle in southern England and found the skeleton of a man who had been killed by a ballista-bolt, was he justified in saying that this proves that Maiden Castle was the site of a major battle between the invading army of Rome, led by Vespasian, in the year following AD43? There is a good prima facie case for saying so, of course, but it is perhaps not the only interpretation of the evidence.

To understand the archaeological evidence fully, it is necessary to see it independently of the layers of history which tend to obscure the picture. This means not allowing historical conclusions and assumptions to run unchecked, examining the evidence at its face value, and attempting to allow the archaeological material to tell its own story. This is not to suggest that the exercise of comparing archaeological evidence with portions of the history of the Roman period as we know it from surviving documents and accounts left by contemporary writers, is unimportant. Links between the two are important and necessary, but the two disciplines deal with different kinds of evidence and help to form different sorts of conclusions about the past.

It is important, therefore, at the outset to examine and define the differences between history and archaeology. Archaeology can be defined as the study of artifacts, buildings, and depositions of material belonging to past ages, and the use of these to build up a picture of man's previous activities. From examination of any kind of material evidence from past societies, archaeologists attempt to gather clues which can help our understanding of social, economic, or, more rarely, political conditions of the time: as objects for study they make use of manufactured products, like pottery and brooches, as well as natural objects like animal and human bones, plant remains, and even deposited soils. Archaeology also embraces certain more specialist disciplines, such as the history of art, papyrology, numismatics, architectural history, and epigraphy. The study as a whole, however, is aimed at the evaluation of the entire physical environment of man, his activities, his effect on that environment, and the conditions under which he lived.

History, on the other hand, is the examination of past events and records, mainly carried out through the medium of the collection and analysis of contemporary source material – whether letters, papers, tax returns, or more formal historical accounts. History is often concerned with narrative, examining motives for actions, and attempting to assess causes which lie behind recorded events. For preference, a proper historical assessment of this nature requires source material which is as closely contemporary and as well informed (and of course genuine) as possible. Within a period as far away from us as the Roman, available historical sources of this kind are patchy, and several are not contemporary with the events they describe. Historical study, too, relies on occasion on more direct evidence – original documents or their surviving portions, inscriptions, papyri, legends on coins – as well as on the less direct record compiled by historians, often themselves benefiting from better access to original documents. All such material has to be carefully examined and its limitations understood. All historical accounts are written from a particular standpoint, as indeed are some other forms of written evidence – such as inscriptions, which can be propagandist. The historian is thus committed to attempt to understand the nature of his source material, the reasons for its compilation, and the standpoint from which another historian's account is written.

Within the terms of these definitions, history and archaeology are separate but overlapping disciplines. Speculation, such as about events whose results may be found within the material evidence on the ground, will often have to make use of historical reasoning. If a wall is discovered blocking off the gate of a Roman frontier fort, historical questions may be raised about why the wall was built. This may in turn lead to the deployment of historical, sociological, or anthropological arguments, and to consideration of whether a change of garrison had highlighted the need for more accommodation space for the guardroom, whether the garrison felt a sense of insecurity, whether there were planning or tactical errors on the part of the Roman army, or whether there was a possibility of increased pressure from hostile neighbours.

Conversely, archaeological study can be of considerable use to the historians, in helping to analyse the nature of their evidence. It may be of significance, for example, to know the source of the stone from which a Roman inscription is cut, to pinpoint its find-spot, or to clarify the circumstances of its discovery. Study of the stone may reveal useful information about where it may originally have been located, the competence of the stone-carver, or what has happened to the stone since it was first set up. This may in turn help to determine the date of the work, or hint at the importance of the message it bears.

Enshrined in Roman archaeological literature are terms which are historically based: archaeologists speak of 'Antonine' occupation layers, 'pre-Flavian' pottery, the Arch 'of Constantine', or 'Hadrian's' Wall. Archaeological finds or structures can often be assigned to, or are by a series of deductions claimed to belong to, a particularly close date-range even within the relatively restricted historical timescale of the Roman period itself. It is perhaps legitimate to ask how helpful this is.

From one standpoint, it can be claimed that the main aim of the study of Roman archaeology is to produce a better and more securely dated framework for each site examined – a further jigsaw piece which can be fitted into historical accounts in our reconstruction of the past. The deductive process – that of linking archaeological finds to precise historical dates – is complex, and is built up on a network of relationships and factors, many of which rely in the last analysis on a correlation between observed archaeological evidence and historically attested dating from Roman historians. The link between particular developments recorded by archaeological means with known historical events is one particularly attractive way of establishing co-ordination between the two disciplines, and there are good as well as bad examples of the way in which it can be attempted. Anything excavated from the remains of Pompeii, for example, which was buried beneath its flow of lava, must date from before AD79. The eruption of Vesuvius which buried the town was witnessed by Pliny the younger, and thus the town's burial can be linked with a secure and unambiguous date from a reliable historical source.

Other historical associations may be far more speculative. It has been claimed, for instance, with far less conviction, that evidence of burning or destruction in the latest phases of Hadrian's Wall is the result of a 'barbarian conspiracy' which the historian Ammianus Marcellinus refers to in a brief account of turbulent events in Britain in AD367. The burden of proof that any destruction recorded at a specific site can be related to a historically recorded event is a heavy one, for if such an attribution turns out to be false, it may throw the whole of a site's chronological framework out of focus. Worse still, if pottery and other artifacts are dated on the basis of this kind of historical tie, their subsequent use elsewhere to impart a similar dating must be of doubtful validity.

This kind of link between archaeology and history is a vital part of our study, but can only be strengthened on the basis of a careful match between finds on site and historical events. This in turn enables artifacts typical of their day to be recognized – those found beneath the lava of Pompeii ought by and large to form a typical cross-section of what was fashionable and available in that part of Italy in AD79. Some areas of knowledge about aspects of the Roman Empire which have a considerable bearing on our historical interpretation have been built up by this kind of careful construction. One such is the study of the expansion and development of Roman frontiers, as shown by the establishment of forts and other military installations, their period of occupation, use, and eventual abandonment in favour of a new location elsewhere. Painstaking study of this kind of evidence takes the archaeologist far beyond mere archaeological conclusions: it begins to point to Roman imperial policies on the wider scale, the stuff of history indeed.

To concentrate too much on the points of contact between archaeology and history may, however, be to miss one of the vital ingredients. If all that can be achieved is to study the Roman Empire solely against the historical backdrop of the Romans' own well-orchestrated view of it, emphasizing its dominance over other peoples and cultures, there is a danger that any conclusions may become blinkered and, in the end, rather sterile. In terms of the development of past societies within Europe, or within even one of Europe's constituent smaller countries, the Roman episode is no more than one remarkable phase – a pattern of change which cannot be fully understood without setting it against what happened before and what happened after it. To do so fully, it becomes necessary to look at archaeological evidence without restrictions imposed on it by the use of Roman historical source material. Instead, breaking out of this mould, and applying properly considered strategies for collecting and assessing evidence, Roman archaeological material can be used to build up pictures of social and economic contacts and indicators. It can point to shifts in population and changes in economic exploitation, help to emphasize the continuity or the discontinuity of life, and begin to document from a far more independent viewpoint the effect of contacts with, dependence on and absorption by Rome.

Even this kind of study will often rely on the traditionally accepted dating for a good deal of Roman material, and could therefore be said ultimately to derive from historical associations. It might seem perverse to do it, but to examine a Roman site in a deliberate attempt not to be bound by accepted datings for Roman pottery and other material would involve a number of 'pure' archaeological processes, some of which are necessary whether or not the material from a site gives a ready chronology to follow.

First, the sequence of development of structures and buildings would be studied and recorded; the deposition of occupation material, and the eventual demise or collapse of the buildings themselves, would be fully analysed according to the principles of stratigraphy – the way in which the soils and other materials were deposited. All the cultural objects found would be recorded and registered as part of the sequence of deposited layers. Study of the deposited layers allows judgements to be made about aspects of the site which are earlier or later than others: a pit may fill up, have one of its corners sliced off by a ditch, which then silts up and later has a well dug through it. The sequence is clear, even though the absolute (historical) dating is lacking. Independently of the site, a start would be made on the collection and classification of material it has produced – pottery, metalwork, coins, bone, and other finds – according to the rather more subjective considerations of typological study. This would seek to define for the pottery, for example, a developmental sequence, worked out according to the shapes of the vessels, the clays from which they are made, the decoration which they bear, the relative quantities of different types, and the clustering, by type or area, of similar vessels. This independent but subjective assessment could then be compared with the find-spots within the site itself which yielded the material, to see to what extent its classification suggested by the typological study matches the recorded sequence in which it was deposited.

Relying on the study of finds from a series of sites whose material had been fully assessed in this way, it would be possible to identify similar or parallel assemblages of material, and thus start to link phases or periods at different sites which may have been roughly contemporaneous. Such an exercise would, in its turn, start to build up a network of further associated material – providing more varieties of pottery, for example, arranged in chronological sequence of deposition in the ground. This could then help to provide a chronological framework for other, different material – brooches, jewellery, or glassware – buried along with it and in relationship to it.

So far, all that has been established for our site is a rough relative

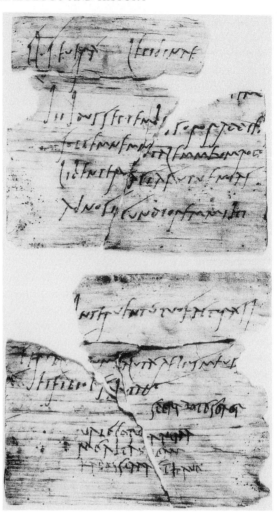

Figure 15 Wooden writing-tablet, dated c.AD100–5, from the pre-Hadrianic fort at Vindolanda, Northumberland. The tablet is a letter from the wife of a neighbouring camp commandant inviting Lepidina, wife of the Vindolanda prefect, to visit to celebrate her birthday

chronology, and although the material is used to determine a sequence, no historical or absolute dating can be put to any of the phases. There is always, however, an understandable urge to assign a historical date of some kind to any site under examination. Where there are no written records and where timescales are rather more extended, as in prehistoric studies, dating can sometimes be achieved through a variety of scientific archaeological techniques, including the measurement of residual carbon-14 within organic material, and cross-checking the results against similar dates derived from the tree-ring sequences of the oldest trees known to man, the bristle-cone pines. For Roman material, however, with a relatively restricted timescale, the imprecision of this kind of scientific dating gives it limited usefulness.

Any desire to deal with Roman material without regard for its historical associations is quickly frustrated by some classes of archaeological evidence. The range of written (and therefore 'historical') records from the ancient world revealed by archaeological exploration of all kinds is great. Prime among these are inscriptions on stone, on papyrus, on pottery, or on wooden writing tablets. Such material can be of any content whatever – from fragments of the writings of ancient authors to official documents or private letters. Other 'documents', too, may take different forms – they are found carved into rocks, within mosaic floors, painted on walls, or punched into sheets of metal, for example the discharge documents which were given to Roman soldiers on retirement from the service. All such finds have an archaeological context which helps to understand them and to enable the message they carry to be interpreted.

Other classes of material bear inscriptions as a matter of course. Roman coins are among the commonest site-finds. These bear a legend from which it is normally possible to determine, to within a year or two, the date at which they were minted. Their study is a discipline in itself, and one which includes examination and assessment of the workmanship of the dies from which the coins have been struck, and their methods of striking, as well as an analysis of the message which they normally bear on the reverse. Because coins provide such a handy and ostensibly well-dated category of finds, archaeologists may on occasion be too ready to use them as an aid to dating the whole site without allowing due weight to considerations which might confuse this apparently simple picture. The date on a coin gives only a date before which the coin could not have been buried in the soil (because it had not been minted by then) and this is not much use unless one can assess the length of time it had been in circulation before it was deposited in the ground. This assessment will be affected by consideration of such factors as whether it was accidentally lost or deliberately buried, or whether, because of its intrinsic value, the coin might have had a long life as savings. Coins from archaeological sites also need to be examined against a backdrop of the overall pattern of circulation and availability of coins within the area at the time, in order to determine whether the site under study has a normal or an atypical pattern of distribution.

The archaeologist meets the written word also in graffiti or makers' names and stamps on pottery or other artifacts. These normally have little 'historical' context as such, but may be very useful in the assessment of standards of written or spoken Latin, or the degree of 'Romanization' which the potters possessed or to which they aspired. The content of such scribblings can say much about the beliefs, fears, or aspirations of the writer: one class of inscribed tablets is the *defixio* – a sheet, normally of lead, onto which a curse is written, before it is rolled up and thrown into a votive well on a temple site in the hope that the requested fate may befall the selected victim.

The study of place-names, important for the Roman period, also links archaeological with historical considerations. Roman place-names are known from several ancient sources – authors, itineraries and road maps, official documents, inscriptions (particularly milestones), and graffiti. It is possible to relate this evidence to known archaeological sites using a variety of techniques. In some cases, this may involve going back through medieval records to find the earliest occurrence of a particular form of a name, and determining by the rules of philological transmission whether this could have been derived from a particular earlier (Roman) name. On occasion, it becomes obvious that a known Roman name belongs to an identifiable place – Londinium, for example, is clearly the antecedent of the modern London – and, once a place has been identified, Roman sources, itineraries, and road-books supply other information which can be used to good advantage.

One such, the Antonine Itinerary, lists the main routes within the Roman empire, with all the major places (and apparently many of the minor ones), even showing how far they were apart, in Roman miles. This should in theory make things relatively simple, for if a Roman traveller took the road out of Londinium towards Durovernum (Canterbury), the itinerary shows that he should first have come, after 10 Roman miles, to Noviomagus, and then, after a further 19 miles, to Vagniacae. The only two known major Roman settlements, however, along this route from London to Canterbury are Crayford, 13, not 10 miles from London, and Springhead, which is 8, not 19 miles further on. The problems of marrying the Roman itinerary with the modern archaeological information are therefore acute. If these known sites are not correctly identified as the two named places from the itinerary, why have two other sites which bore these names not been discovered? Alternatively, if one assumes that these two sites are those which the itinerary lists, is it legitimate to emend the text of the Antonine Itinerary to make its account consistent with the situation on the ground? Such problems as these, which can be found right across the Roman world, are compounded when, as is the case in most areas, written sources give a variety of names (not necessarily always in the same form for each apparently individual place) with no indication of where they actually lay, and which cannot be assigned, without a great deal of surmise, to any particular site.

Finally, archaeology and history combine in the Roman world in descriptions by Roman writers of places, buildings, or objects which are still identifiable today. These, too, are diverse – from the detailed description of the layout of a Roman camp by Arrian or Polybius, to the remark by the late Roman writer Ausonius that the city walls of Tolosa (Toulouse) were built of brick, as excavations have confirmed. Pliny, in his *Natural History*, mentions a particular form of prized and expensive drinking vessel, much beloved of wealthy men in the first century AD,

Figure 16 Fluorspar cup from Turkey, probably a *vas murrinum* as described by Pliny (photo Ashmolean Museum, Oxford)

known as *vas murrinum*. From his description, we learn that these were made of some form of natural mineral substance, lustrous rather than brilliant, with a variety of colours, but particularly purple, white, and red, producing a rainbow effect. They were soft, and could be nibbled, and they imparted a pleasant odour to wine drunk out of them. Pliny's detailed description enables the archaeologist of today to define these *vasa murrina* as fluorspar cups, three examples of which are known to have survived from the Roman world. If those that survive can be closely linked to Pliny's description, it would give a date for the vessels, though this is a more dangerous argument, and the popularity of such cups (or their value as antiques) could have meant that they were much prized also at times other than the period Pliny describes.

In practice it is virtually impossible to close one's eyes entirely to the correlation between archaeological evidence and historical sources. Links have to be established between the material found and the world which the Romans themselves described, and these serve as pegs on which to hang a series of more or less precise dates for the finds from an excavation. The link is, however, more fundamental than this. The archaeologist will normally expect to examine a site in any given area against some form of background framework for events in and development of the area in the Roman period, derived either from historical sources or from informed hypothesis – 'model building' – about how human and economic processes in the area were at work. Unless the site is approached in this way, research questions about the material found or about the significance of the discoveries may not be correctly posed. Yet this form of hypothesis or assumption in its turn may make the task of evaluating the site all the more difficult. The accepted picture of the history or archaeology of an area may on occasion colour the interpretation of a new site.

As an example of the potential dangers here it may be instructive to take the case of destruction attested at the Roman site of Corbridge at the end of the second century AD. On excavation, it was discovered that there was a substantial layer of debris across major areas of the site, and material associated with this can be assigned to the date-range AD160–80; none of the material need date from any later than 180. It is always tempting to relate the signs of what appears to be such an obvious piece of destruction with enemy action, and, on examination of the available literary sources, reference is found to a raid by one of the local barbarian tribes on this particular frontier in AD197. A link is thus made – Corbridge was burnt down in 197 as part of the devastation on the northern frontier caused by the raiding by the Maeatae. Such a ready link may seem attractive because of the easily assimilated historical frame-work it gives, but it fails to take account of all the questions which may arise. First, can the destruction on this site be definitely related to enemy action, rather than, say, an accidental fire or a radical change of building plans? If the destruction of the site is unquestionably caused by enemy action, is this necessarily related to the historically attested raid? There is nothing in the archaeological evidence which says that it cannot be: but our historical sources for events in northern Britain are partial and selective, and they may not have mentioned every hostile event which might have caused destruction on this scale. If we allow that Corbridge does bear the results of the raid of 197, there is a danger that others will take this assumption as a fact, and that the group of material which was broadly indicative of a date around 180 will later be taken as a group which is distinctive for the attested date of 197. Within the relatively close date-ranges for Roman material, this sort of potential misdating could lead to all sorts of false historical conclusions.

Conversely, when viewed on its own, archaeological evidence has to be carefully studied. If a number of north British sites on the Roman frontier have traces of destruction, burning, or demolition which appear to belong to the same date (from the types of pottery, coins, and other finds buried within associated deposits) there is a case for arguing that they are the product of a series of enemy actions which formed part of a concerted attack on the whole frontier. This is particularly true when the historical sources provide a series of pegs in the form of attested raids by hostile forces on which to hang the network of theory. Such associations, once made, tend to become crystallized as accepted 'facts', forcing additional later finds which may be slightly discordant, and which ought to force a re-examination of the basis for the original theories, to be fitted in to support them rather than to provide the essential reassessment. This is not to suggest that the history of a Roman frontier written in such a way is always wrong: conclusions derived from archaeological evidence in this way require continual rethinking and revision in the light of fresh evidence.

Historians and archaeologists use their material in different ways even within the normal confines of their own disciplines. Roman history can be

studied by treating ancient authors and texts as the most informed version
of what actually occurred or how life in the ancient world was lived. It is
thus possible to construct a view of Roman civilization without recourse
at all to archaeological evidence. Using this source material alone, one
could examine such subjects as the way the Roman civil service worked
and the family background or racial origins of the men who served in it,
judge social attitudes of the Romans to other races with whom they came
into contact, or, by relying on more specific sources like the writings of
Josephus or the New Testament, gain an appreciation of the way of
Roman life in general in Judaea in the first century AD.

It is also possible to interpret data from the ancient world in the light of
economic, sociological, or anthropological trends. Rather than concentrating merely on evidence which showed how the civil service worked,
this might mean reading between the lines to try to determine what
Roman civil servants were attempting to achieve and why, whether their
attitude to their work was socially motivated, what they felt about it, and
what people's attitudes were towards them. To study a subject such as
racial prejudice in the ancient world, one would need not only to look at
the ways in which non-Romans are represented in individual authors
(who, after all, represent only a single voice each), but also at the
occurrence of Roman and foreign names on tombstones, inscriptions, and
other documents, at evidence for separate religious rites and practices
and for the existence of separate communities, and to make some
estimation of the peoples from whom Romans felt themselves racially or
culturally different. This stark ancient evidence must then be matched
against a modern view of what would count as evidence or manifestations
of racial prejudice, in order to judge it fully against a backdrop of
sociological or anthropological considerations.

Archaeological data, too, can be viewed in more than one way.
Conclusions are derived from observed data in a quasi-scientific fashion,
relying for dating on a complex network of associations with other
material, and for events on the interpretation of the traces in the ground.
Thus 'this building burnt down in AD180' is a crystallization from all kinds
of evidence relating to what constitutes a building, what it would look like
if it had been burnt down, and the host of associated material
contemporary with it, and pre- and post-dating it, which helps to bracket
its period of occupation and use, and allows the date of its end to be
assigned. It may only take the reassessment of a single piece of the
assembled data – the realization that a certain type of pottery found
within the building could not have been in circulation until some years
later – to upset a number of archaeologically derived historical conclusions. It would not be true to imagine, however, that the complex web of
pottery dates and typology can be expected to undergo such upheavals
very frequently. The study of some types of Roman pottery – both

empire-wide wares like *terra sigillata* and more local forms – has resulted in the possibility of relatively accurate dating, to within 10 to 15 years. Other types of pottery can at present offer less accuracy. Problems of interpretation derive not so much from the date of manufacture of these wares, as from the date they were deposited in the ground and the length of time prior to that they had been in current use.

The complete excavation of any site is a flash of light, which at least in theory provides a glimpse of a fully documented sequence of develop-ments at the site under examination. Take the example of a Roman villa, whose domestic buildings, field systems, stockyards, and barns have all been minutely examined and recorded. Some people may be tempted to view this as a 'type-site', a good, well-researched example of a villa which can be held up as a model of what a typical Roman villa was like. Seen in this light, the evidence from the site assumes, for modern eyes at least, a greater significance, and modern studies may give it prominence over other sites in the region precisely because it is so much better known. Without some means of comparison with neighbouring sites, however, there is no way of knowing whether this evaluation is a balanced one.

The problem of comparison with other sites is in itself difficult. If valid conclusions require detailed evidence, and if there is no other comparable site near to our villa which attains anything like the same standards of excellence of recording, recovery of material, or analysis of the data, many of the more general conclusions reached about Roman villas in the area have to rely upon evidence derived from the one villa where the facts are well established. At best, it may be possible to compare our villa with others elsewhere in the Roman world which have been excavated to a comparable standard; but since these may lie in widely dispersed places, where the agricultural regimes in antiquity may have very little in common, and where the social backgrounds may have differed greatly, the value of such comparative study is limited.

One method of solving this impasse might be to compare the development of this well-excavated villa with other sites in the neighbourhood where the evidence is defective, to determine to what extent conclusions about prosperity and decline, growth and retrench-ment observed at the first villa can be matched or traced as part of the general pattern of the immediate area, or, more speculatively still, as part of the overall development of the province within which it lay. Alternatively, it may be possible to concentrate on a specific aspect of villa studies – e.g. the extent to which the implantation of Roman villas (and probably also the farmland estates which went with them) respected or cut across earlier pre-Roman land-uses. Examining a specific theme like this might enable the researcher to reach conclusions about the process of Roman development of the area, making use of both the solid evidence from the excavated villa and the less comprehensive data from other forms of reconnaissance.

These, and a host of similar, broader questions based either on the villa itself or on material found at it, are avenues which the archaeologist may wish to explore. Many pieces of evidence can be used: the villa's plan and layout (when compared to others), the construction, rebuilding, and expansion of its buildings, the size and layout of its field systems, or the overall extent of the estate. In addition, from the finds at the site it may be possible to make some estimate of its environment, its farming and stock control practices, and its inhabitants – their diet, their standard of life, their physical shape, their fears and beliefs, or their prosperity. All the finds from the site will go in some way towards the formation of this sort of picture. When broadened to other sites of comparable type and date, such considerations form much of the main thrust of Roman archaeology.

The greater part of such a study relies on evidence of quality from the site or sites concerned. What makes archaeology a particularly demanding discipline is the fact that the exhaustive study of a site using archaeological excavation techniques of necessity removes the possibility of ever repeating the exercise. As a site is excavated, the deposited layers are carefully distinguished, recorded, photographed, and sifted to extract the maximum possible information, and then removed. Every attempt is made to ensure that the processes which have resulted in the deposition of each individual layer of soil are properly understood. Records are kept of the types of material excavated, the extent of each layer, and their interrelationship. The information recorded about the site is as accurate as can be achieved. The site, after all, must be regarded as a historical document which is in the process of destruction in the cause of reading it thoroughly.

The key figure therefore in the whole exercise is the excavation director. It becomes the director's burden to be responsible for the controlled destruction of the site: at the same time a heavy responsibility and a privilege. Everything depends upon the professionalism of approach and the skills of the excavation team. If the quality of their recording is not of the highest, they may provide incorrect information on which to base balanced judgements about the site in the future. The site will thus have been destroyed without the full potential for providing understanding about it and its place in the past being realized.

It is necessary, therefore, for the archaeologist to be equipped with every possible assistance, first, to record and understand the site under examination and, second, to make available sufficient details about the site to record what was found and to enable their own personal view of the site's interpretation to be substantiated, as well as giving scholars, archaeologists, and historians of the future a basis for their own understanding of it, albeit necessarily at second-hand.

Archaeologists are sometimes criticized when they seek to stamp high standards of professionalism upon the subject they serve. They can be accused of attempting to stop amateurs from enjoying their 'weekend digging' on favourite sites, of seeking to prevent metal-detector operators from searching for and collecting artifacts from the ground, or of being unduly concerned about unprocessed and unpublished excavation work from past decades still languishing in the archives. When one views these concerns, however, in the light of the fact that only information gained from excavations carried out with adequate resources to cope with all aspects of the task will produce results which can be relied on, the affair is set in perspective. There will always be misgivings about inadequate excavation, however enjoyable to those participating, about the removal of finds located by metal-detectors from contexts in which they were laid down in antiquity, or about the irresponsibility of approach to their discipline by those who seem to be unwilling (for whatever reason) to make available to others the results of their findings.

In addition to these considerations, and the heavy burden of responsibility incumbent on the director of an excavation, there is a further requirement. It is not sufficient merely to record as competently and as accurately as possible what is being discovered on a site under excavation. It is absolutely necessary at the same time to interpret and understand it. While excavation is under way, decisions have to be taken about the strategy of the task; these can depend in large measure upon the developing understanding of the way in which the layers of the site have been deposited. Although much of the fine detail often remains to be added at a later stage after thorough examination of the written records and the finds, the structural sequence (for example) has to be understood while the site is in the throes of excavation. All the more reason to demand a high degree of professionalism and competence from the excavator of a site.

Thus archaeological evidence is not always as simple and clear-cut as one might imagine. In order for it to be of fullest use in determining what has happened in the past, it needs to be comprehensive, accurate, fully digested, and evaluated. Other archaeologists therefore have to assess any excavation which they come to study at second-hand, and give its facts and conclusions a relative value: this is tantamount to the suspicion with which historians would approach the writings of one of their sources. The historian, on reading Tacitus's *Histories*, will want to ask why he wrote them, what made him choose to relate particular episodes, and whether he had some ulterior purpose in writing about what he did. If so, this may affect the value of the historical picture of the times which he portrays, but it may also assist in giving a deeper understanding of the political or social climate of the day.

In a similar fashion, the archaeologist, approaching the published report of a site, must ask why the excavator chose to explore this site. What were the expectations or hopes with which the site was approached? Was the projected research design a reasonable one? More controversially, the evidence presented and the conclusions derived from it must be scrutinized – was everything that was found fully recorded, was the significance of any of the evidence missed, and can all the conclusions about the site be fully substantiated?

Archaeological data are of necessity about the individual and the particular: the study of a building here, a coin-hoard there, a group of pottery or artifacts from somewhere else. Only by collecting all this material, by assessing its strengths and weaknesses as evidence, can more general conclusions be hinted at. It can rarely tell us what individuals thought, relate to historical figures or events, or show the consequences of historical actions. Rather it provides the backdrop to the pattern of life in the Roman world. Its mass of data can be assembled, sorted, and used to address a variety of questions. Answers may be more limited and tentative than we might perhaps like (and possibly than many readers of this book would suspect), but at least, given solid data, a serious attempt can be made to form valid conclusions about the nature of life in antiquity. In the next few chapters, I hope to show how various forms of archaeological evidence have been and can be used to form impressions of the Roman past.

5

The archaeology of
Roman architecture

Before considering the evidence which can be gleaned from buried
Roman remains, it is worth attempting to review what can be learned
from an archaeological study of Roman architecture. There is a surprising
number of surviving standing buildings of the Roman period. Some, like
the Pantheon or the Colosseum, are virtually whole, or, if only partial,
still impressive. Others have only traces of their foundations left, from
which an impression of the original design can be formed – for example
the Temple of Vesta in the Roman forum. The survival of Roman
buildings can be the product of several different circumstances. For a
start, they were normally substantially built, and have therefore remained
in use, though not necessarily for the purpose for which they were
originally intended; a fragment of the baths basilica at Leicester known as
the Jewry Wall has survived because it was incorporated into St Nicholas's
church in the Middle Ages. Others have survived through the very impres-
siveness or usefulness of their structure, as is the case of the aqueduct at
the Pont du Gard, the aqueduct at Segovia and the bridge at Alcantara in
Spain. Others still, like the walls and gates of a variety of towns and cities
of the empire, among them Rome, Autun, and Barcelona, have survived
because they were kept in use as the boundaries of Roman, post-Roman,
or medieval cities.

Other traces of Roman buildings have been revealed through
excavation, and their remains exposed to the world for the first time in
recent centuries. Of particular value for the study of Roman architecture
has been the excavation of well-preserved buildings discovered at
Pompeii, Herculaneum, and Ostia. These have added a sample of an
important and diverse range of town houses and other urban buildings to
chance survivals elsewhere. It is scarcely likely that buildings in a
similarly complete state of preservation lie awaiting discovery in many
other places. The excavation of buildings in order to recover their
ground-plan, however, has proved a worthwhile exercise, and can
contribute significantly to the study of Roman architecture.

Roman architecture is of particular importance because of its
interlocking relationship with developing styles of artistic expression. This
is especially the case where a building bears a wealth of decorative detail,

63

or sculpture, as part of its overall design. This has led to an understandable concentration on objects or buildings whose prime purpose appears to have been commemorative and monumental rather than purely functional. Thus, to the historian of Roman art, the Ara Pacis Augusti or the Arch of Trajan is of greater interest than one of Frontinus's aqueducts which brought great quantities of water into the city of Rome, or one of Trajan's frontier fortresses. The study of a decorative and commemorative monument like the Ara Pacis clearly affords far more scope for the exercise of an evaluation of its artistic contribution, and for assessing its position within the wider subject of the historical development of Roman art.

Such an assessment, however, relies on a modern view of the surviving legacy of Roman monuments and buildings. Unfortunately, we know little about the Romans' own view of their artistic abilities and architectural achievements, although we have to assume that those buildings which do survive can be taken as an accurate reflection of the artistic and architectural tastes and trends of their time. They may have appealed to the tastes of either the Roman populace themselves or, perhaps more likely, those patrons who commissioned and paid for buildings to be erected. Whilst these latter might on many occasions have ordered particular designs or made use of forms of decoration which were able to impart the desired political message, on other occasions they may have been content, within certain limits, to allow craftsmen and stonemasons to exercise artistic expression. In any such assessment allowance has to be made for the extent to which economic influences were at work in the Roman period: on occasion, the lack of funds may have seriously inhibited the level of artistic achievement.

Part of the discipline involved in the study of Roman architecture lies in an art-historical approach, in which the appearance of various forms of decoration and other stylistic traits, including overall layout and design, are treated historically and typologically. The aim is to arrive at a framework which can serve as a basis for assigning dates to buildings and to elements of decorative art in general, and thus contribute to an understanding of the chronological and stylistic development of Roman art in all its forms. In order to achieve this, it is necessary to relate the detailed study of each surviving or well-recorded Roman building to the historical and documentary evidence for its construction date. This will enable elements of the design or the styles of Roman architecture – the decoration, materials, or techniques – to be placed in a securely dated progression. From this, one can determine the sorts of styles and techniques which were current at any particular period. This period in turn can be placed in an ordered progression within which other buildings, not dated by documentary evidence, can be fitted by matching their surviving stylistic and decorative details to their correct place in the established sequence.

It will be necessary to study each building in some detail to do this properly. Archaeological analysis must identify its original plan or design, together with any Roman or post-Roman alterations or additions. Straight joints, changes in the style of building, or breaks in the construction technique may show that it has been altered or replanned, and further clues may be given by the materials from which it is made, or its overall design and techniques of construction. Any decorative elements forming part of the structure must be correctly related to the sequence of development of the building. It is important that any such study is thorough; if the building is only superficially understood, or if its historical development is confused or falsely interpreted, any conclusions drawn from its study will be of doubtful value.

After forming an outline sequence for the stages by which a Roman building has reached its present condition, it is necessary to look at the historical evidence. It may perhaps bear an inscription attesting its construction, its dedication, or rebuilding at some particular time. This has to be carefully examined. Can an inscription always be relied on to tell the historical truth, or are there elements of propaganda – e.g. a false claim as to who erected the building – about it? It will be necessary to assign the inscription to its correct phase within the building's history: here its positioning or find-spot, even the material from which it is carved, may be vital. Of particular importance will be to determine whether it was part of the original design of the building unaltered by later architects, or whether it had been moved later to its present position.

Other types of historical evidence can also be used. References by contemporary writers to buildings which they saw and described can be used as indicators that a certain building – perhaps otherwise undated – was in existence at a certain time. Coins and medallions on occasion carry representations of buildings – sometimes apparently to commemorate building or rebuilding – and there are also sculptural friezes or paintings which enable individual buildings or elements of towns or cities to be recognized. Finally, there are some surviving contemporary maps and plans of elements of Roman cities – the marble plan of Rome, for example, or the cadaster plans of Orange. These give a detailed if partial breakdown of the city plan at a particular moment in its history, and this can be of considerable use in determining the layout of the ancient city-scape. All such material must be assessed as carefully as possible: written descriptions of buildings need to be matched with surviving remains.

More fundamental as a relationship is the task of assessing the original function of a building from its form. It may seem ridiculous to question

Figure 17 The Pile de Cinq Mars, a Roman tower on the north bank of the Loire between Tours and Angers, Built primarily of brick, its upper regions are decorated with panels of geometric patterns; its purpose is unknown

the assumptions we make about the form and function of a forum or a temple, an amphitheatre or a bath-block, all of which are relatively well known and sufficiently distinctive. There are many examples of Roman buildings, however, whose function is considerably less assured, or whose identification rests on little more than inspired guesswork. The Pile de Cinq Mars stands in the Loire valley, close to the junction of the Loire and the Cher. It is a massive, solid, brick-built tower, some forty metres high, with four curious turrets at its peak. It bears panels of decorative mosaic work which have some similarities to other decorative schemes on Roman buildings elsewhere. Its materials are Roman, but it is of totally unknown function, and, as is the way when buildings are not understood, it is usually assumed to have had a funerary or commemorative purpose. Not knowing its function, however, makes it difficult to compare accurately with other structures, for we may not be comparing like with like. If we know what it was used for, a building can more easily be classified according to a known scale of values, parallels, and relationships to others; a building whose function cannot be understood is difficult to study meaningfully.

After amassing all the possible historical clues to the function or the date of our buildings, it remains to study them type by type, probably also region by region, and to attempt to form a sequence first of all of those whose construction date can be pretty well assured. By analysis of the plan, design, the detail of decoration and moulding, it is possible to understand how ideas and tastes changed over a period of years, and well-attested and dated buildings can be deployed as markers along a line of development. Once this line is sketched out, other known but undated buildings of similar form and function can be matched against it, and their position within it assessed. Thus an approximate dating can also be given for them.

The major difficulty for such a programme is the conservatism of Roman taste over several centuries. We are familiar with the plan and layout of a Roman temple, and this did not alter significantly throughout the imperial period; a theatre always looked like a theatre, triumphal arches do not radically alter in design from one end of the Roman period to another. Only occasionally, as is the case to some extent with Roman fortifications, does the whole pattern of Roman architecture change to any marked degree: from the turf and timber of the early campaign forts to the standardized layout of the stone-built playing card shaped fort of Trajanic times, and the final appearance of much more irregularly planned and heavily defended smaller fortifications in the later Roman period. It is thus in most cases difficult to see a meaningful sequence of alterations in the plan and layout of buildings alone. More can normally be gained from consideration of the ornamental detail on them: the style and form of the columns and their capitals, or the form, richness, and combination of the friezes and other decorative details.

The typological approach of which this is an example has its own dangers. The basic premise of a typological series is that there is a gradation in any artifact from the simplest to the most complex: the idea was developed in the 1860s by Pitt-Rivers, initially from his study of musketry, but he then applied it to prehistoric objects, firmly basing his analysis on Darwinian ideas about evolutionary principles. According to this view, an object was made to be used, and its design or decoration was continually improved and altered in accordance with an increasing sophistication and a search for improved efficiency. If we now arrange the material according to this principle, it should produce a type-series in chronological sequence.

Whereas this may work to some extent for buildings, too, it cannot be guaranteed to be foolproof. Does it necessarily follow, for example, that the simplest and least decorated temple will be the earliest, and that the largest and most elaborate the latest of any given sequence? Or is it necessarily the case that the basic two- or three-roomed house in the countryside is always the very earliest of villas, whereas the ninety-roomed mansion is always the latest? There is a significant difference between many forms of building and the sorts of artifacts which Pitt-Rivers was studying to develop his view of typological sequence: artifacts, by and large, can be carried around and have a reasonably wide distribution. Buildings, on the other hand, are static, and their influence on design of other buildings elsewhere is not necessarily great, unless there is some linking factor between the two areas in which they are found.

One example of buildings which can confidently be claimed to form a coherent series, within which the same influences were brought to bear, is the rock-cut tombs of the Near-Eastern Roman and Nabatean city of Petra. By the early fourth century BC, Petra was the ancient capital of the Nabateans, a desert people, but it came under Roman control in the latter part of the first century AD, and was in AD106 annexed into the Roman province of Arabia. Although the city itself was extensive, the most obvious modern-day survivals from the Nabatean and Roman periods are a series of rock-cut façades, mainly those of tombs, which are scattered in the hills in the neighbourhood of the city. These are not strictly Roman architecture, for they draw on the motifs and practices of Egyptian, Assyrian, and classical Greek traditions. The façades range from what appear to be the earliest simple rectilinear decoration, a single or double groove above a doorway, to a pedimented entrance surmounted by a façade with cavetto mouldings. Others, even more elaborate, and thus, one might assume, later, have a doorway flanked by pillars, the whole surrounded by a grander pillared façade bearing a single or double cornice. Among the most elaborate is the Corinthian

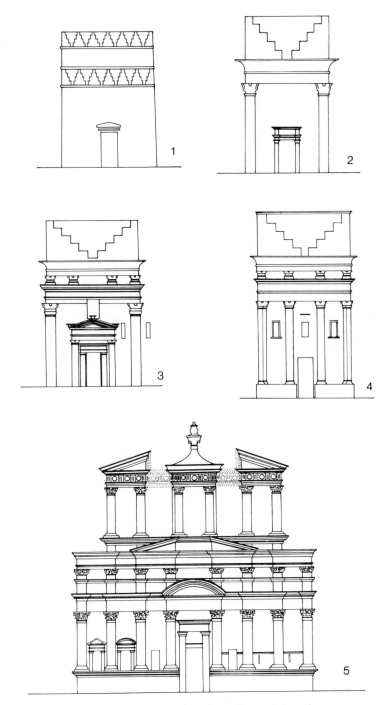

Figure 18 Temple façades of tombs at Petra; 1 Assyrian type;
2 Cavetto type, with a cornice supported by a pair of columns;
3 Double cornice type, a more elaborate version of no.2;
4 Classical double cornice; 5 Full classical type – the Corinthian
Tomb

Tomb, which unfortunately survives in a rather damaged state, but which once was clearly a completely different design and seems to be closest in style to the most elaborate of the surviving tombs, the Treasury (Kasneh). Both of these completely abandoned the crow-stepped cavetto mouldings, and embraced classical forms. The Treasury tomb is fronted by six massive columns which support a shallow pediment and cornice, but is also surmounted by a further register of columns, supporting a broken pediment on each side, but forming a small circular independent building at its centre. This, it appears, may date from the first century BC. The Roman contribution, when it came, was to build on the accepted framework of the Nabatean tradition, and to be sensitive to the existing monuments of the city which they had come to control. This typological development of tomb façades cannot be readily dated; although there are differences between various styles which suggest differing periods of construction, the periods merge gradually, and the monuments cannot therefore be placed rigidly according to type along a measured sequence.

In the study of buildings, as of other classes of ancient evidence, one can also apply a reverse typology. To assume that a designer, artist, or craftsman is always striving for the best may not be realistic. It is possible that there will be examples of poor workmanship or less elaborate design alongside the best that the Roman craftsman could produce. If one views the typological sequence as progress towards a degree of perfection, there has to be a point where the curve of standard of craftsmanship drops off again. After its peak, the form of a building may become simpler, corners may be cut in the style or the standard of workmanship, construction methods may become quicker. Occasionally, too, craftsmen may have tried to copy some example of a building which they failed fully to understand, and thus the design may be misunderstood or the decoration misapplied.

One of the most obvious cases where this applies is in the skill of carving inscriptions. Experts can tell from the style of lettering on an inscription what is its date of workmanship, using other examples of similar lettering styles, and any other available indications of date, including the occurrence of known figures, names, and formulae within the message carved on the stone. The close relationship of dated inscriptions to a clear development of lettering styles has meant that examples of inscriptions which bear no attested date can be assigned in many cases to a relatively close date-range. Opinions vary, but it is generally agreed that the most perfectly formed inscriptions occur in the early second century, under the reigns of the emperors Trajan and Hadrian. From then onwards, the art of letter-cutting, spacing, and the satisfying shaping of the letters themselves become (to modern eyes at least) less polished, until, by the fourth century, inscriptions have more of the appearance of earlier cursive handwritten script than the well-spaced

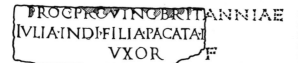

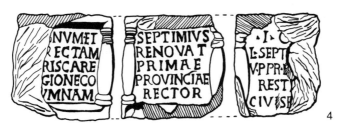

Figure 19 Roman inscriptions from Britain, showing different lettering styles of different periods: 1 First century, from London; 2 Early second century, from Wroxeter; 3 Mid–late third century, from Caerleon; 4 Fourth century, from Cirencester

regular Latin of the honorific inscriptions of earlier days.

On occasion, rather than develop a fully integrated typological sequence of buildings or decoration types, it appears quicker and easier to seek a site which presents a parallel for the one under study. Any element of a building – its plan, layout, function (where this is known), or stylistic components – can be compared with other examples of similar buildings elsewhere. Thus, in studying Roman fortifications, it can be tempting to cast around the Roman world for all the known examples of polygonal projecting towers, however far-flung they may be – at the sites of Cardiff, Oudenburg (Belgium), Turin (Italy), Burg-bei-Stein (Switzerland), or Split (Yugoslavia) – and postulate a similar date for them all. Unless the individual examples, however, can be closely dated themselves, and their relevance to each other demonstrated in some way (other than merely having the same plan which could be produced by chance), it is hard to see precisely what conclusions can be drawn from the identification of sites like this which look the same. It is scarcely possible to draw any conclusions, e.g. as to date, from the presence at different sites of similar features unless, for example, in this present case there is some other factor to explain why the construction of polygonal towers on a fortification at one site should have been linked with that at another.

If from their design or architectural style they do not readily provide a historical context into which they can be fitted, buildings can often be dated by archaeological means. Every standing or ruined building has an archaeological history. Deposited floor-levels, foundations, and construction trenches can be examined and excavated, irrespective of the size or grandeur of the surviving remains. All forms of archaeological evidence can be used to assist in this form of dating – pottery, coins, or other artifacts discovered in the foundation trenches, and which were current at the time the foundation trenches were dug and open. Alternatively, or in addition, a structure can sometimes be dated by reference to material beneath it; if a building lies above deposited layers, its construction date must be later than or roughly contemporary with the latest datable object within those layers. Material found in such a position, however, gives only a *terminus post quem*, an earliest possible date.

Buildings also sometimes contain clues as to their date as a result of the materials from which they are constructed. Various scientific techniques (pp.138–9) make it possible to date timbers from the accurate measurement of their tree-rings, or hearths and furnaces from the magnetic imprint left within them when they were fired to high temperatures. The use of other types of materials – brick, tile, marble – can sometimes be seen to have been in fashion, perhaps while the materials themselves were only available at a specific period when the factory or quarry was in production or under exploitation. Bricks or fired clays can be dated by means of thermoluminescence (see pp.123–4) or may bear makers' stamps. The use of bricks bearing stamps enables us to date the construction of the basilica at Trier to the reign of Constantine (AD306–37). Tiles which formed part of the walls of Rome built by Aurelian between AD271 and 275, however, also bear stamps of the time of the emperor Hadrian, some 150 years earlier, and show that such evidence can only be treated as a date after which the walls were built. Other older material, too, can be found forming part of new structures, and helps fix a date for them. Many of the city walls of the Gallic provinces have their foundation courses composed of large blocks of stone culled from a variety of sources – temples, city monuments, tombs, or milestones. Some of these can be dated from the style of lettering on the inscriptions they bear, or the style of carving of the decoration; others bear dated inscriptions, and there is a particular group of milestones found within the walls of the city of Rennes, all of which date from the third quarter of the third century AD.

Artifacts of all kinds can be discovered within walls and other structures – fragments of pottery and coins, perhaps dropped by builders during construction work. These are rare finds, and it appears that all too often coins found merely in the proximity of walls and other structures have been uncritically taken as imparting a date to the structure itself. The exact find-spot of such coins or pottery is vital: it must be determined whether these are found embedded within material integral to the construction of the walls, or whether they are part of the accumulated debris round them consequent upon their collapse. Any such information can then be given its proper weight to help fix the date either after which the wall was built, or after which it must have collapsed.

Buildings can be dated from their relationship with other structures. Some can be assigned dates according to their position within a development of a town or an area of an archaeological site. At Pompeii, for example, various portions of the town were developments added at definable periods; temples and houses within these areas can therefore be assigned dates according to their context. Certain types of site – cemeteries in particular – tend to spread in a measurable progression. Along a street leading out of the city, those tombs nearest the city gates would be expected to be the earliest, while those furthest away might be the latest. A later Roman Christian cemetery, on the other hand, might spread outwards in definable steps from a central shrine or from a martyr's tomb, thus giving an observable sequence of growth. It is rare, however, to be able to examine a sufficient portion of a town or cemetery, or a frontier fort and its associated settlement, to enable all such nuances of developmental sequence to be recognized and fitted into the historical pattern of the site.

From this it can be seen that archaeology can on occasion provide an essential check to help determine whether the art-historical analysis of the buildings is on the correct lines, and to spot the conscious archaisms, the

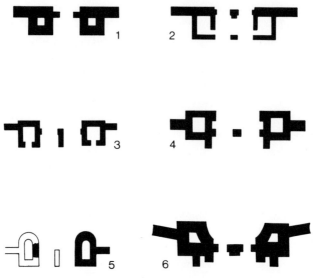

Figure 20 Plans of Roman fort gates: 1 The east gate at
Wiesbaden, *c.*AD90; 2 The west gate at Housesteads,
*c.*AD125; 3 The north-east gate of Pförring, *c.*AD141; 4 The
south gate of Carnuntum (legionary fortress), AD188 or
later; 5 The east gate of Passau, early third century; 6 The
west gate at Carnuntum, AD188 or later

innovations, and the re-use or incorporation of outdated materials. It also
enables a history of construction techniques to be established, where
these can be identified and their application understood, as well as
identifying what building materials were available at various periods.

There are, as always, some notes of caution to bear in mind. There is
no guarantee that a sequence of development plans of a building type
which holds good for one area of the Roman world is also applicable to
another. It may often be true that styles and developments at Rome or in
the emperor's home province led tastes and fashions elsewhere; but the
empire was also wide enough to incorporate elements from the many
different cultural traditions which it met in the provinces, and to create
new amalgams of styles and achievements which allowed each area to
develop separately and independently of any central controlling influence
other than the most general.

Even in those areas where a strong central authority may be assumed
to have been in command, there are still an astonishing number of small
differences of detail in the design of buildings. Many layouts of fort
gateways are known, based on the theme of a pair of entrance passages
flanked by towers. The shapes of the towers, the amount by which they
project from the fort walls, and their sizes show considerable variations

on the theme. If arranged typologically, they might encourage the assumption that the gates and towers of the earliest forts were the simplest – that they did not project from the walls, and had the simplest square or rectangular form. This view, however, is not entirely borne out by the archaeological evidence, and the general principle, even if it is allowable, fails to take sufficient account of divergent developments in different frontier zones where localized and individual designs seem to have been produced at various dates.

The most powerful and wealthy architectural patron in the Roman world was the emperor himself. Imperial projects therefore were most likely to produce changes in design and plan, and fresh adaptations to new needs. This is certainly the case on the imperial frontiers: where the emperor was actually present, far more construction work seems to have taken place. Some emperors had a reputation for making their troops work hard in peacetime on a variety of architectural and engineering projects. Many of the most adventurous building projects in Rome or in the provinces took place as part of schemes executed for the emperor himself – for example the imperial fora, the succession of palaces built for the emperors at Rome and elsewhere, or such adventurous schemes as the construction of the Amphitheatrum Flaviense, the Colosseum, on the site of what had been a lake in the grounds of the Palace of Nero.

Engineering and technical developments within the architectural profession were fundamental to the level of civilized life which the Roman expected. The careful planning and layout of roads and harbour-works, the provision of adequate water supplies to towns and cities, and the furnishing of machinery for mining and other industrial processes, were all major concerns which helped to assure high levels of trade and economic prosperity in the Roman world. In considering Roman architecture it is necessary to take an overall view of developments in these engineering fields as well as what we would regard as the more traditional province of the architect; the Roman architect would have dealt naturally with both.

The development and sophistication of techniques and processes of engineering were often essential concomitants of the demands of empire. The exploitation of ever more difficult seams of metals, demanding more sophisticated pumping and extracting gear, was necessary in order to keep the army supplied with weapons, and to produce a stable coinage with which to pay the troops, among others. An adequate water supply was regarded as essential for a town, city, or fort, and some of the most elaborate and elegant survivals of Roman architecture – the aqueducts of Segovia in Spain, and of Nîmes in France (the Pont du Gard) – were a product of the engineering which went towards this provision. The road system tapped other constructional skills – those of choosing the correct line for the layout, the laying of a permanent base and a surface finish to withstand the weather and demand the least possible maintenance, the crossing of natural obstacles such as rivers or hills with bridges or tunnels. By studying the development of Roman engineering techniques, no less than architecture itself, it may be possible better to appreciate the interrelationships between these physical elements and the administrative structure and history of Rome. Such study should also give a different slant on parallel developments in mainstream architectural practice.

Our knowledge of the history of some of the best-known Roman buildings often relies upon the most equivocal of evidence. The Maison Carrée at Nîmes is one of the best preserved Roman provincial temples. It stands on a platform 3.3 m high, and is 26.4 m long by 15.55 m wide. It has columns on all four sides, six across its width, and eleven along its length, of which eight are attached to the side of the body of the temple itself. The temple is generally acknowledged to be purely 'classical' in style; its fluted columns have Corinthian capitals, and the entablature bears a flowing frieze on three sides, with, on the fourth, the space for an inscription. It stands in a colonnaded courtyard at the centre of the city, and for that reason it has been suggested that it was the *Capitolium*, the main city temple or Capitol, in a close relationship with the main forum area.

Important Roman temples within a city area might not only be sacred to one of the gods or goddesses of the Roman pantheon, but might also be dedicated to a member of the Emperor's family. The date of the Maison Carée, the deity to whom it was devoted, and the question of whether it was also set up in honour of some other person have been matters of debate for some considerable time. The inscription on the main front of the building has disappeared; it was in bronze lettering attached by small dowels to the masonry behind. Only the holes to take these bronze dowels now survive. These show that there was once an inscription of two lines, one of which took up all of the upper register, the other shorter and occupying only the central portion of the lower part of the entablature. In 1758, a survey of the fixing holes for this inscription suggested to M. Séguier that it was a dedication to the two grandsons of Augustus, Gaius and Lucius Caesar, who were adopted by him in 17BC:

C · CAESARI · AUGUSTI · F · COS · L · CAESARI · AUGUSTI · F · COS · DESIGNATO/PRINCIPIBUS · IUVENTUTIS

This reading, however, failed to take account of all the holes which had been recorded within the inscription space: in 1834, it was suggested that the inscription referred not to Gaius and Lucius Caesar (as the 'Princes of Youth') but to Marcus Aurelius and Lucius Verus (who also took that title), but the first letter of the inscription would then have had to be M, and there seems to be little space to fit this in. The suggestion that all the

Figure 21 The Maison Carrée, Nîmes

available fixing holes had not been used in the accepted reading of the inscription found another champion in 1919, when Espérandieu proposed an alternative reading, which he suggested had been an earlier inscription supplanted by the one to Gaius and Lucius Caesar:

M · AGRIPPA · L · F · COS · III · IMP · TRIBUN · POTEST · III · COL · AUG · NEM · DAT ·

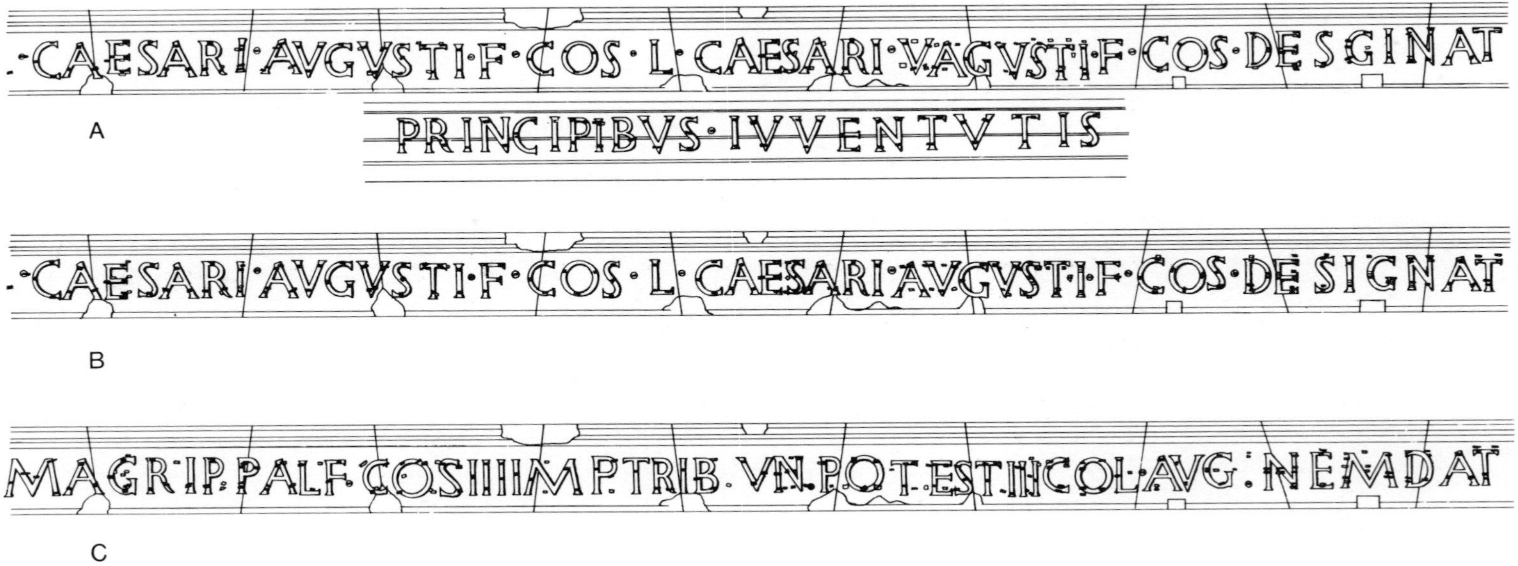

A

·CAESARI·AVGVSTI·F·COS·L·CAESARI·VAGVSTI·F·COS·DESIGNAT

PR·INCIPIBVS·IVVENTVTIS

B

·CAESARI·AVGVSTI·F·COS·L·CAESARI·AVGVSTI·F·COS·DESIGNAT

C

MA·GR·IPPA·F·F·COS·III·IMP·TRIB·VIN·PO·TEST·II·COL·AVG·NEM·DAT

Figure 22 The inscriptions on the front of the Maison Carrée Nîmes; the black dots and circles represent bronze dowels or dowel-holes cut into the masonry. A The inscription as first set up, with masons' errors (e.g. VAGUSTI for AUGUSTI); B The straightened and corrected version of line 1; C The suggested reading of Espérandieu for line 1: note how many of the holes are unaccounted for on this reading

These theories have led to the view, still to be found in several modern sources, that the temple was built by Agrippa (around 19BC or a trifle later), and that it was rededicated in AD1 or 2 to the two young princes, Gaius and Lucius Caesar. Re-examination of the temple in 1964–8, including a minute study of the fixing holes for the inscription(s?), has led to a broad reaffirmation of the original reading of 1758. Most of the holes which fail to fit in with this reading can be convincingly explained as mistakes in the placing or alignment of the bronze letters by the mason who was charged with the work – one of the letters seems to have been placed upside down when the inscription was first set in place! According to this interpretation, not only do the letters of the inscription themselves have their dowel holes in a constant position in each letter of the alphabet, but also certain of the visible scribing marks on the stone behind can be seen as corrections of mistakes made when the first set of holes was cut for receiving the letters. There is still one problem; the very first letter of the inscription must, on this interpretation, have been a C, but there is no extant fixing which would support this letter, and a dowel hole at this point obviously does not relate to a letter C. This has not yet been convincingly explained.

Close examination, therefore, of the settings and fixings for the letters of the inscription has established that its most likely interpretation is as a dedication to Gaius Caesar as consul and to his brother Lucius as consul designate for the following year. The year that fits is AD1, when Gaius was consul at the age of 23, and his brother due to hold the office in AD2. If this inscription was part of the original building, and not added to an existing temple, this gives a firm date for the construction. The suggestion that it was built by Agrippa some years earlier, though still not impossible, cannot any longer be substantiated by the evidence of the dowel holes which supported the inscription.

It remains to consider the deity to whom the temple was sacred. If indeed it stood within the forum of Nîmes, it may well have been the Capitol, and therefore dedicated to the Capitoline trilogy. However, there is no sign of the internal divisions which would have then been necessary. Whatever the original dedication, it is likely that on the unfortunate death of Lucius, at Marseille in AD2, and of Gaius, who died two years later, the honorific gesture was made rather hastily – perhaps even during the construction – to dedicate it to the two young Caesars. One can therefore assume that the temple is dedicated to Rome and the imperial family, though this is no more than a 'best guess'.

Archaeological examination of the Porta Nigra at Trier has considerably enhanced understanding of this spectacular city gateway, notably during restoration work carried out between 1970 and 1973. Trier (Augusta Treverorum) developed in the first and second centuries AD as an open and unwalled Roman city. In the course of time a substantial

Figure 23 The Porta Nigra, Trier, with Simeon's Gate, from the east, in an engraving of the mid-nineteenth century. Note the projecting semicircular tower of the Roman gate (to right), with its large inverted U-shaped windows between engaged columns. The other tower projecting towards Simeon's Gate is of early twelfth-century date

circuit of walls was added. Archaeological observations suggest that these walls were built no earlier than the second half of the second century, since to the north of the city they cut through a cemetery of first- and second-century date. At the other extreme, literary sources tell how the gates of Trier were shut in AD353 against Decentius, the brother of the emperor Maxentius; the walls must have been built no later than that date.

The Porta Nigra is the northern city gate, and it is on a grand scale. It is a double-portalled entrance, flanked by a pair of projecting semicircular towers. Within, there was an unroofed courtyard, gated towards the south. There is no provision for gates on the outer archways, though a portcullis slot survives. The gate is built of massive greyish-green sandstone blocks without mortar and held together by iron cramps, set in lead channels; this made it a very popular source for metal in the early Middle Ages, and it owes its survival through this period to its adoption by a hermit, Simeon, as his cell in 1028. After his death, it was converted into a church established by Poppo, Archbishop of Babenberg; most of the Roman structure, with two storeys of arcading above the gate passages, and a third storey in the towers, was retained, though at some stage the east tower lost its top storey, and there is an eleventh-century apse added to the east end.

It is claimed that the Roman masonry shows signs of never having been finished; many of the stones were left with large rusticated bosses: the engaged columns are only roughed out, not given a final polish, and the contractors' marks, some of which show that the third storey of the west gate tower was built in three weeks, have not been smoothed off. The doors do not seem to have been hung as planned – the channels into which they were to open have not been properly dressed back: some of the decorative detail in the inner courtyard does not accurately fit. All this, the product of detailed observations, has suggested to some scholars that the Porta Nigra was built in a rush, and that the scaffolding used to erect it had had to be struck before the job could be completed. This view led in turn to the assumption that the gate was built under the threat of the arrival of an invading force, and to the search for a suitable historical episode for its construction which could add substance to the evidence from the building.

The apparent shoddiness of workmanship also led to the assumption that the gate must date from the later third or the fourth century, and for many years the Porta Nigra was by definition 'late Roman'. The archaeological context of the gate, however, shows that it was contemporary with the foundations of the city wall. These foundations are most likely to date from no later than the final thirty years of the second century. This archaeological dating does not help to explain the incomplete state of the gateway, but the thorough analysis of the gate's

Figure 24 The remains of the granaries at Corbridge, Northumberland, seen from the north end

structure has enabled it to be assigned to its rightful place within the framework of Roman architecture, and has helped to bypass the fruitless search for a historical context for the construction of the gate as a method of providing a clue as to its date. However, it has still not resolved all the enigmas posed by the apparently incomplete state of the gate, the reasons for which may never be known.

One of the areas where the relationship between archaeological analysis and architectural forms is most acute is in the skill of producing reconstruction drawings. Among the best preserved of the buildings at Corbridge, the garrison town near Hadrian's Wall, are a pair of stone-built, buttressed granaries, first excavated in 1907–11. They lie side by side, their long axis north–south, and with columned porticoes at their south end. They survive to a maximum height of about 2.4 m (8 ft), which is just a bit higher than the level of the Roman floors within them; these were raised above a series of under-floor ventilating channels, served by mullioned air-vents between the buttresses. As they stand at present, the granaries were probably built in the Severan period, but they rest on the foundations of a pair of granaries planned and apparently

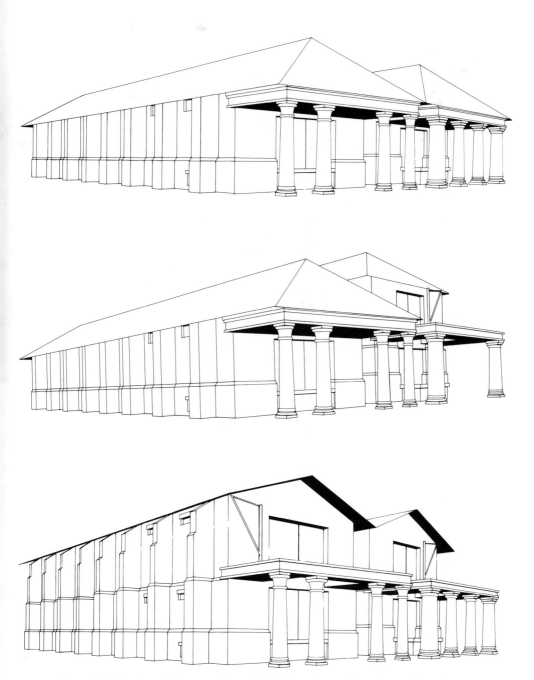

Figure 25 Sketches of the granaries at Corbridge, drawn from the south end, showing three versions of how they may have been built. The upper portions of all the drawings are conjectural, as is the idea of loading platforms above the columns fronting the pair of buildings

begun some twenty-five years previously, and which were never completed.

Before reconstruction drawings of this pair of granaries were attempted, several forms of evidence had to be combined. First, the standing masonry had to be examined in order to understand the form of construction, observe the style of the stonework, identify details of the construction – for example the existence of a chamfered plinth course running round the buildings at a height of about 2.4 m from ground level – and make an estimate as to the height of the roof (from the level of the internal flagged floor). Second, plans drawn by the excavators of the buildings earlier in this century are an important source for determining whether there were once other details or fragments of evidence, no longer visible, which needed taking into consideration. Third, the buildings' surroundings, including the drainage system, gave important clues about the form of the roof. The granaries are encircled by a drain which collected water from an eavesdrip to west and east, and which carried the flow round the south front of the buildings via a covered drain under their porticoes. A short spur drain collected water from a short stretch between the two granaries, but, because they are set so close together, one must assume that for much of their length the roofs must have touched, and been provided with a valley gutter. If this was indeed the case, it in turn suggests that the two roofs were of the same height.

When examined carefully, evidence from the porticoes is by no means straightforward. Each is of four columns, and there is no visible means of collecting water which may have run off their roofs. The column bases lay at different levels – the outermost columns of the east granary corresponding with the base of the granary – but all the other column bases lay at least 0.35 m (1 ft) higher, suggesting that they were not contemporary.

The sketch reconstructions here show an attempt to take some account of all these points, though none of them is completely satisfactory. The first shows a pair of single-storeyed granaries, their roofs brought forward 'Swiss chalet' style to form the porticoes. The treatment of the buttresses, with chamfered courses at two levels, looks more medieval than Roman, but is a piece of modern-day bias which should be ignored. Bringing the roofs forward to the line of the porticoes in this way would have substantially lessened the weight carried by the columns but it is hard to see what was the purpose of the porticoes.

The second drawing seeks to explain a series of seven large blocks set centrally in the lower levels of the east granary. These have variously been described as supports for a timber roof span or for stone vaulting, or as the underpinning for an upper floor. The drawing shows a suggested two-storeyed east granary, which has much in common with surviving stone buildings at Ostia and Rome. The porticoes in this scheme would have functioned as covered loading bays for the ground floor and as loading platforms supplied with pulleys for the upper floor. This drawing attempts to show a suggested phase in the life of the granaries – it is mere speculation – but does fit several of the observed facts, notably the different foundation depths of the portico columns. The sequel to this is shown in the third drawing, which shows the western granary brought up to the same height, more columns added in the porticoes, and both granaries now complete with loading platforms and covered bays.

Consideration of these three individual buildings in France, Germany, and Britain shows how fundamental it is, for a correct interpretation of a building, for assessing its date, or for attempting to show what it might have looked like, to have an accurate survey or informed and thoughtful observation of the structure on which to base archaeological interpretation. Without this, theories may be formed which have no weight, and conclusions of specious authority can be reached which gain acceptance merely by being repeated. A thorough and professional archaeological appraisal must have a solid grounding in hard fact, and be consistent with all the available evidence. It is thus important to treat Roman buildings, whatever their state of preservation, as archaeological artifacts, with their own context, and containing their own clues as to function, date, and significance.

This example demonstrates that there may be several different ways, each of them consistent with the archaeological evidence, in which the remains of a building could be restored to give an impression of how it appeared to the Romans themselves. In this case, it may be that the building itself was altered during its lifetime, so that no single interpretation is necessarily the correct one. In other cases, there may be considerable debate about the appearance of the upper portions of a town gateway or a country villa. The excavated ground-plan and other evidence from the site may give a firm basis on which to build ideas of how the rest of the structure was finished. These will probably reveal the positions of fireplaces and hence chimneys, identify preserved traces of the material from which the roof was made, and, if the building collapsed *in situ*, give clues as to where the windows were or what was the height of the walls. Even so, a great deal of conjecture has often still to be used in completing an accurate drawn reconstruction.

This is of particular concern when the reconstruction of a Roman building is in stone and mortar at full scale rather than a sketch on paper. In order to satisfy visitors' thirst to know what the often scrappy remains uncovered at ground level really looked like in the Roman period, there can sometimes be a temptation to go in for full-scale restoration. Sometimes this is limited to a column or two resurrected from where they were discovered lying flat or a portion of a roof built to provide needed protection for more delicate remains and to enable them to be displayed

Figure 26 The main south gate of the fort at the Saalburg, Bad Homburg. One of
the most famous reconstructions of a Roman building, this was built for Kaiser
Wilhelm II between 1989 and 1907

in as reasonable an environment as possible. In some cases, however –
and remains of the Roman period seem to be more prone to this than any
other – the desire to interpret for the visitor has gone considerably
further, with the reconstruction, in their original positions, of buildings of
which no more than the mere ground-plan survives.

One of the first such Roman buildings to be given this treatment was
the Roman fort of the Saalburg, near Bad Homburg in Germany.
Excavation of the site was thorough, and showed that there had been a
fortlet on the site prior to the implantation of a permanent fort around
AD135 and abandoned about AD260. The excavation's patron, Kaiser
Wilhelm II, provided funds for the rebuilding of portions of the stone
fort. The complete circuit of walls, including all four gates, as well as
some of the stone buildings within the fort – the headquarters, the
granaries, and part of the commandant's house – have all been rebuilt to
something like their original form. The remainder of the fort's interior
now looks much like a park, though it would originally have been covered
with barracks, workshops, armouries, and stables, all of timber. Only a
single pair of such buildings have been reconstructed, and these are not in
their correct position according to the Roman layout.

This reconstruction is now more than seventy years old, and is itself almost a monument of the past in its own right. In certain respects, the evidence it contains for how Roman forts looked is a little out-of-date – further consideration might need to be given to the design of the gates, the form of the crenellations or of the rampart walk, and some of the interior buildings have problems of guttering and drainage which would have had to be solved by the Romans if they were to keep foodstuffs dry. There are, however, other more modern projects on an equally ambitious scale, including another in Germany to rebuild portions of the major town of Xanten, just south of Bonn. Here in recent years parts of the amphitheatre, the town walls, including one of the major gates, and one of the temples discovered by excavation have all been rebuilt according to the best modern assessment of how they would originally have looked, and using only those methods and forms of equipment which would have been available to the Romans. As an experiment and a learning process about some of the problems which were faced and solved by Roman engineers and technicians, this is doubtless very valuable (though presumably also costly), but the whole process must fill the archaeologist with a certain amount of unease.

First, there is the problem of authenticity. The remains of the Saalburg, largely rebuilt in the decades before the First World War, are not genuine Roman work, and yet they may form for many people the most enduring impression of what a Roman fort looked like, and throw into particularly stark contrast the poor and fragmented state of other sites where rebuilding has not taken place, even though these may be much closer to the genuine remains of Roman workmanship. It is surely important that we do not allow ourselves to be so carried away with reconstructing Roman remains that it becomes possible to lose sight of the value of what is genuine.

Second, all such projects have to rely on a degree of conjecture. If it were proposed to rebuild one of the major medieval abbeys on the basis of the existing remains, there would be substantial problems of knowing how to complete the roof lines, which period of the abbey's construction to work to, and all sorts of compromises would doubtless have to be met. The same is true of most Roman sites, except that with only a ground-plan available for study, a rather simpler view, and possibly a freer hand, is possible. In the case of the granaries at Corbridge, however, no single full-scale reconstruction would be totally satisfactory or could do justice to the complex history of the building which can be read from the existing remains. While conjecture can be harmlessly indulged by studying the remains and producing drawings or paintings which can help to bring them to life, it is a different thing altogether to clothe one of the fancied interpretations of a building in stone, timber, brick, or even earth, and to make of it a permanent statement of what that building or structure looked like.

It cannot be denied that, in terms of their attractiveness to visitors, reconstructions of this sort can make a powerful statement. They can show the physical presence of a building or can give an appreciation of its internal 'feel' far more immediately than is possible with any number of drawings, paintings, or even computer-generated graphic displays. These educational benefits, however, must always be carefully weighed against the potential damage which grafting a new structure onto an old one may cause, and against respect for and full understanding of the original Roman structures themselves. It would be unfortunate to hand on to our descendants a legacy of Roman remains so heavily overlaid by our own possibly mistaken interpretations of them that it is impossible to undertake any meaningful reassessment.

6

The archaeological examination of Roman sites

Sites where Roman material lies buried in the ground can be identified in a variety of ways. They range from the well-known and obvious places – the major centres of the Roman world – to limited or minor sites of indefinable type, whose presence is known or surmised only by a tell-tale scatter of coins or pottery. As the clues to a site's existence vary, so also do the methods that the archaeologist can use to detect and assess them. The processes of deduction about the existence or the extent of Roman sites may on occasion seem little more than inspired guesswork. There is far more than this, however, to the skill of interpreting what lies under the ground, and clues as to the nature of archaeological sites can be gained from several different sources.

One of the clearest indications of potential buried remains comes from those places where Roman buildings and masonry still stand above ground level. The survival of masonry, however, does not automatically provide clues to either the complexity or the extent of buried associated structures or deposits. In some cases, where for example a city wall survives, as at Silchester in southern England, it is obvious that remains of major buildings lie within the walled circuit, and in fact this is known from past excavations and spectacular aerial photographs which show the parched lines of buried foundations. Even so, a substantial proportion of archaeological material relevant to the history of the town of Silchester lies outside the city walls – elements of pre-existing boundaries, the cemeteries, and the site of the amphitheatre.

Conversely, at a site such as Wroxeter, the standing portion of Roman masonry which lies within the circuit of the now obscured but still traceable town defences has been recognized as Roman for many years. Without research excavation at its foot, however, it would have been virtually impossible to guess that it forms part of the baths basilica. Other enigmatic elements of Roman masonry still await fuller explanation and context. As examples one can cite the substantial defences round the apparently remote site of Iruña, in northern Spain, the pile of stones known as the Temple de Janus near Autun in France, or the substantial complex of buildings, thought to be the remnants of a villa, which still stand to a remarkable height at Thésée, in the Loire valley.

Figure 27 The remains of the Roman villa at Thésée, near Montrichard in the Cher Valley, France

Equally clearly identifiable Roman sites are the known cities, towns, fortresses, or forts of the Roman world which lie beneath and have formed the foundation for modern-day places. Among these can be numbered sites such as London, Lisbon, Paris, Sofia, Bonn, Vienna, Bucharest, Budapest, Belgrade, and Rome itself, to name only those European capitals which had Roman predecessors of one form or another. In many, if not all of these, occupation since the Roman period has been virtually continuous, and the Roman levels lie buried under a substantial build-up of the debris of occupation of later periods. This means that excavation of their Roman phases, if it takes place at all, is of necessity expensive and complicated. The remains of succeeding periods have to be recorded and removed archaeologically before Roman deposits can be reached at all. There is also a good chance that layers of Roman material may have been considerably disrupted as a result of the superimposition of later buildings, the foundations of which may have cut through them. In addition, there is always the consideration that if, as is not unusual, Roman material is buried up to 10 or 15 feet deep, this very depth can entail complicated problems of engineering and logistics if the deposits are to be examined archaeologically, thus adding considerably to the expense of the operation.

Excavation within a big city can be an extremely expensive and frustrating business: the site available for excavation, necessarily limited by modern-day constraints, cannot be guaranteed to bear any close relationship to the Roman city layout, and may therefore not contain the whole of a building under examination. The time allotted for excavation work, normally in advance of building development, may be short due to business deadlines and cost. Sites for examination have to be carefully chosen: the impact of relatively modern foundations and basements on the buried and superimposed layers has to be assessed as far as is practicable. When excavation work on such sites is envisaged, and when funding to carry it out is sought, it is often necessary to determine in advance – perhaps by commencing excavation in cellars, or by drilling bore-hole cores and examining the layers the drills penetrate – whether there are important remains in the area under examination. Roman towns, though by and large smaller than those of today, were not necessarily as highly urbanized. Substantial areas within them, therefore, might never have been built up, even though enclosed within the city defences. Although negative evidence of this sort is very valuable to the scholar, the costs of excavating a large hole to a considerable depth to find little or nothing of the period under examination cannot be said to make the exercise an attractive one.

There are serious difficulties, therefore, in the examination of the Roman period in such urban centres. Almost by definition, these were among the most important places in the Roman world, but the presence of modern buildings and the consequent pressures on these sites for development and change make their examination or preservation very difficult to achieve. What is more, Roman levels and buildings may be buried beneath remains of other very significant periods, about which much more needs to be known. When there is a limited timescale for excavation, therefore, these periods and levels may rightly be given priority over those of the Roman era. It is thus necessary to acknowledge that remains of these later periods – the medieval, Saxon, Viking, Carolingian, or 'Dark Ages' – all of which will normally lie closer to present-day ground surfaces than the Roman levels and which therefore stand more risk of being disturbed by modern development, should be examined thoroughly, and possibly in preference to the Roman material. Remains of the Roman period, particularly if they are so deeply buried that they will not be affected by the foundations of new structures, may perhaps not need to be examined at all. Although this will deny satisfaction to modern inquisitiveness about this period, there is some consolation in the fact that by being sealed undisturbed under modern developments their preservation for future generations to study is being secured with little or no harm done to them.

There is another paradox connected with the study of the major centres of the Roman world. As it is normally the case that the Roman towns or cities were much smaller than their modern-day successors, any associated suburbs, outlying settlements, and cemeteries may lie buried under relatively modern growth. If the Roman city was a market centre which attracted a string of smaller settlements, farms, villas, and agricultural estates within a reasonable market-day's travelling distance of its centre, then these elements of its economy, too, are likely to lie under the sprawl of developed urban villages and suburbs round the modern centre. Despite modern suburbs not being so heavily built-up as the city itself, such elements of the Roman rural pattern will still be difficult to examine archaeologically; opportunities for excavation in the suburbs of modern cities may not be all that frequent, and the chance that development and growth in the area has damaged the Roman features is all too likely. The prospect of obtaining a complete picture of the economic and market patterns of a major Roman centre of this type is thus far from promising. If such a piece of research can be undertaken, it will probably be expensive.

Obviously it is vital, as part of our understanding of the period, to know more about the most important Roman centres, about the rural economy which supported them, their country estates and field systems, so that as complete a picture as possible of Roman life in them can be built up. It could be argued that such study could more easily, and with more likelihood of little or no post-Roman disturbance, be carried out on a Roman centre which no longer forms the focus of a thriving urban development. Here other forms of archaeological survey and prospection could be employed to examine the Roman landscape and context with a greater expectation of forming a complete picture at considerably less cost.

More types of archaeological prospection than can be employed in urban settings are as a rule available for sites in rural areas. The survival of earthwork remains dating from the Roman period – the traces of earth-and-timber fortifications, of ditches and ramparts, or of the ruins of buildings which lie where they fell and have by a gradual process been covered with earth – afford the prospect of field survey and interpretation of what lies under the ground from the surface remains. The survival of sites in this sort of condition is relatively rare in Europe, apart from in areas of the upland zones of Britain, where there are some surprising surviving remains, mainly of the Roman military occupation of the area. These include the earthworks and buried remains of forts and their ditches, as at Ardoch, in Scotland, marching camps at Cawthorn, in Yorkshire, practice siege camps at Burnswark in Scotland, and buildings in the settlements surrounding the forts at Housesteads on Hadrian's Wall

Figure 28 Cawthorn Camps. An aerial view showing the series of four camps, probably of late first- or second-century date at Cawthorn, North Yorkshire

Figure 29 The Roman practice camps and siege-works at Burnswark, Scotland, from the air

and at Old Carlisle in Cumbria. These remains, however, are rivalled in one or two other places: a series of Roman burial mounds survive at several points along the Roman road from Tongres, in Belgium, towards Köln: Roman marching camps of the Republican period can be seen at Numantia in Spain, and thoroughly remarkable remains of the Roman period are clearly visible at many places in the desert lands of the Near East and Africa. Whether these should be considered as survivng buildings or as earthworks is perhaps a matter of definition. The surviving camps which housed Roman troops engaged in the siege of Masada, Herod's fortress in the Israeli desert, and the evidence at the site for the effectiveness of Roman siege tactics are a striking practical counterfoil to the practice measures to be seen at Burnswark.

Many archaeological sites are by no means as clear-cut or as easily definable as all these examples. Antiquarian records and accounts sometimes mark the find-spot of pottery, coins, or sculptures of Roman date revealed by chance at a particular location: local museums may contain material brought in at various times, which, when their find-spots are plotted on maps, begin to show a concentration of material from a particular area. New finds can add confirmation to earlier accounts or produce evidence to show that a completely new site may have been discovered. On occasion, the existence of a Roman site is a secret known to very few people: a farmer may be well aware that a particular part of his land is more stony than others, and may therefore lift his plough over buried foundations and rubble so as not to damage them. Users of metal detectors may find that the ploughsoil in one particular zone is more productive of coins and other objects than elsewhere. Field work, normally taking the form of walking over freshly ploughed areas collecting and assessing the density of pottery sherds and other material recovered from within the topsoil, may show a concentration of artifacts coming from one particular place, and, allied to other evidence, could give clues as to the kind of site which lies buried there. Other clues to the existence of a site come from records of Roman place-names, where these are given in ancient itineraries. The whereabouts of Roman sites and settlements, not now easily traceable, may be initially surmised from such sources, and examining the topography or field-walking in the vicinity of Roman roads or at suspected points may also bear fruit.

All such methods of discovering new sites are of great importance in compiling a picture of the past and attempting to study the overall settlement patterns within a given area of the countryside. Much depends on the reliability and comprehensiveness of the information base. Some people may have their private reasons for keeping the existence or their discovery of a site to themselves. The surviving 'bank' of archaeological sites of the Roman period is a finite resource, however, and a comprehensive record of them is a priceless source of information about the Roman past if it can be analysed and studied in its entirety. Many archaeological sites are not of first-rate importance; but information about each one can be seen as a small cube of mosaic which, when arranged with all the others, helps to create a fascinating and comprehensive picture. Most countries have efficient local museums and repositories of information about archaeological sites which act as a first source of information about their location and what is known to them. It is important that this database of information is kept up to date and as well informed as possible by anyone who can assist.

The fact that a Roman site has been discovered and partially studied or excavated in the past not only confirms its mere existence, but can also indicate the potential for further information retrieval by excavation. The scale of previous excavation work is always of great importance: most excavation of the nineteenth or early twentieth centuries will have concentrated on only the most obvious buildings or floor-levels, and the degree of disturbance and disruption which the site has suffered as a result of this will need careful assessment. In many cases, antiquarian researchers because of their method of following Roman walls in an attempt to determine the ground-plan of the building, may have removed some of the most important associated layers from the archaeological remains, or may have dug through the site in a haphazard and unplanned way. Often this kind of exploration will have led excavators to dig through later layers, containing less solid or less obvious traces, without recognizing them in their search for solid walls or floors.

The villa at Dalton Parlours, near Leeds in Yorkshire, was first examined by excavation in 1854. At that time, the foundations of the main house, of winged corridor plan, were cleared, and the first of two mosaic pavements at the site discovered. This, featuring the head of Medusa, was lifted and taken into a nearby museum. The site was backfilled and agricultural operations continued over it. In 1976, local archaeologists, alarmed at the apparent erosion of the site by the continual ploughing, which turned up fresh debris on the surface of the ploughed fields, mounted a full-scale excavation, partly to check the nineteenth-century plans, and partly to see what was left of the site to salvage.

The results were far more interesting and productive than the earlier excavation might have led one to believe. The Roman villa consisted of a main house with several ancillary buildings, including a separate baths-block, a well-house, and a substantial aisled building containing rooms with an underfloor heating system and a corn-drying kiln, all arranged within an irregular walled enclosure of about 1.2 ha. Recovery of finds was poor due to the severe abrasion of the site by ploughing, but material dating from the second century was sparse, and was in complete contrast to the relative abundance of third- and fourth-century material; little was discovered in stratified contexts above or within the villa buildings. There was evidence of occupation of the site in the post-Roman period, dating possibly from the seventh or eighth centuries. The surprise discovery, however, and one which could not have been deduced from the earlier excavations was that the villa lay almost exactly on the site of a farmstead of Iron Age date and type. This was formed by a series of looped ditched enclosures within which there were round huts of differing dimensions. Three sides of the ditched enclosure round the Roman villa followed the ditches of its Iron Age predecessor.

Other Roman sites are described in historical sources, and can be identified from contemporary or informed accounts left by Roman writers. One of the most spectacular of these is the desert fortress of Masada in Israel. The Roman historian Josephus describes how in the Jewish revolt under the emperor Vespasian in AD73, the Zealots withdrew to the desert and were followed and besieged by the Roman procurator of Judaea, Flavius Silva. Josephus records that the rebels

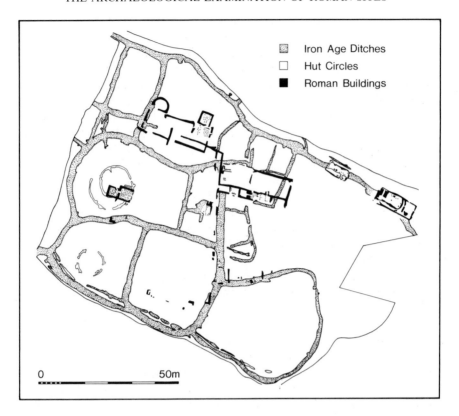

Figure 30 Outline plan of the villa at Dalton Parlours, near Wetherby, Yorkshire. The Roman buildings are shown, as they survived modern plough damage, above the outline of a series of Iron Age enclosures, some of which contained huts. For the sake of simplicity, many of the post-holes, probably forming part of other Iron Age structures, have had to be omitted from this plan

withdrew to the site of Masada, described as a flat-topped rock with sheer sides, to which there were two very difficult paths, one of which was known as the 'snake' route. Jonathan the High Priest had built a fortress on the rock, and this had been rebuilt by Herod. Round the top of the hill there was a wall 7 furlongs in length, built of white stone. It was 12 cubits high and 8 cubits broad, with 38 towers, each 50 cubits high. Most of the top of the hill was good land, and was used for crops. A palace, containing courtyards, pillared colonnades, and mosaic floors, was built at the western ascent, within the citadel, but on the north side. An additional feature of the fortress was the pits and reservoirs dug in the rock to retain all available water, and the large tower built to dominate the entrance path, making it almost impregnable; huge quantities of corn, wine, oil, pulses, and dates were laid up inside the fortress.

Josephus's account of the Roman action against Masada tells how the Zealots, the *sicarii*, fled with the Roman army in hot pursuit to the hilltop, under the command of Eleazar. The Roman general Silva immediately undertook a siege, building a wall all the way round the hill so that none of the defenders could escape. Selecting a spot for his assault at the so-called 'white promontory', he built a mound 200 cubits high and raised a further mound of stones on it. The dramatic course of the assault was also recorded: an iron-plated siege tower was raised on the mound, and, under its cover, the wall round the top of the hill was breached. The defenders, however, managed to mend the gap with an earth-and-timber baulk, but the Romans set fire to this. Under cover of darkness, and now defenceless against a renewed Roman attack, the 960 defenders decided that they would rather kill themselves than fall alive into the hands of the Romans. The only survivors, when the Romans stormed a strangely silent citadel the next morning, were one old woman and five children who had taken refuge in one of the cisterns, and thus escaped the general massacre.

The name Masada was linked in 1838 to a hilltop site in the Israeli desert previously known as Es-Sebbeh, and subsequent travellers, writers, and explorers reassessed and refined the arguments for that identification from the surviving remains on the hill, until the site was excavated in 1963–5. The foot of the hill is ringed by the remains of a wall associated with eight camps of typical Roman design and plan, and of varying size. A massive ramp strikes obliquely upwards virtually to the summit of the hill on its western side: this seems to be the mound raised by the Roman legion (X Fretensis) in AD73. On top of the hill, traces of buildings were clearly visible before excavation. As excavation progressed, it became clear that there had been a massive casemated wall round the circumference of the hill, with storehouses and rock-cut cisterns within it. At one point a synagogue was discovered: at several others, remains of palatial dwellings, including a swimming pool, culminating, on the northern slopes of the hill, in a dramatic palace built at three levels.

The remarkable coincidence of archaeological discoveries with Josephus's account leaves little room for doubt that the excavated site of Masada is the site of the siege and suicide of the Zealots. There was little sign, however, of the actual events of that fateful night; twenty-three skeletons were found in a cave below the brow of the hill, but it was not possible to determine whether these bodies were those of Zealots of AD73. Similarly, the discovery of a series of pottery sherds (ostraka) marked with names including that of the leader of the revolt, finds an echo in Josephus's story that the leaders of the Zealots drew lots as to who was to carry out the slaughter. Such finds as these, though not

Figure 31 Aerial view of Silchester, showing the street layout and the traces of some of the stone buildings as cropmarks

necessarily a conclusive demonstration of the historical events, come possibly as close as archaeology is able to the actuality of the historical story, and certainly call forth an evocative response from the excavator and the visitor.

One of the most important methods of discovering and examining new archaeological sites is aerial photography. Many types of site can be seen from the air to good advantage: a complex earthwork site may well become more understandable if its plan and context can be seen at a glance, and the significance of some of its features can often be most easily grasped from above. Flying can also enable the archaeologist to carry out initial surveys of large areas relatively cheaply, in order to determine whether any other features of particular interest merit further detailed attention. Large areas of desert in Syria, Jordan, and Algeria were searched earlier in this century by pioneers of aerial photography, in an attempt to document the surviving traces of Roman frontier systems and forts. These photographs, taken by Baradez in Africa, and by Poidébard and Mouterde in the Near East, now form a valuable archive of material in their own right. Many of the sites they discovered and recorded may not yet have seen any further archaeological survey or examination, and the photographs themselves are an eloquent record of the state of survival of these sites as first recorded and documented.

Fortunately aerial photography is not limited only to the prospection of earthwork sites or standing buildings. At various times of the year, dependent upon weather conditions, a growing crop can show traces of archaeological features which are deeply buried and therefore invisible on the surface of the field it occupies. Broadly speaking, this happens in one of two ways: either by the parching effect of buried walling producing a 'negative' cropmark, or by displaying more luxuriant growth above deeper deposits to produce a 'positive' cropmark. Parching occurs when walls, floors, or any hard surface – e.g. a roadway – lie buried near the surface of a field. In any sustained spell of dry weather, a crop planted in soil which overlies such features may not obtain sufficient water to survive, and may thus wither and die, revealing the outline of walls and floors as parched marks in the field. Often the effects of the presence of buried walls are not so dramatic, but may show up in slightly stunted growth or a quicker rate of ripening of any crops planted above them. At certain times, and maybe for only a matter of a few days in the growing season, a contrasting colour can be seen from the air, compared to the remainder of the field. Conversely, a 'positive' cropmark occurs when a crop is planted over the richer and deeper soil of a filled-in feature like a ditch. Because its roots are healthier and have a deeper supply of humic deposits than are available in the surrounding field, the crop here produces a more luxuriant growth, and will usually ripen slightly later, than the remainder of the field. Thus for a few critical days, normally in late summer, there is the chance of spotting filled-in pits and ditches from the air from the slight – or sometimes dramatic – colour differentials in the ripening crops.

The view from the air can also show sites in cultivated land in other ways – different colourings in the soil may show the sites of buildings (from the spread of construction debris) or of ditches (the extent of a darker humic deposit), particularly after ploughing. One spectacular result of observations of this kind has been the discovery in the Somme basin of northern France of a series of Roman villas. Here complete ground-plans of some of the villas have been traced and photographed from the marks of their white chalk foundations outlined in the dark soil of the fields after the plough has tracked backwards and forwards across them.

Aerial photography is clearly a major benefit for the archaeologist, but it has its limitations. The landscape rarely bears traces solely of the Roman period – it bears the imprint of many different uses to which men have put it, and sometimes, too, the traces of natural or geographical features. Cropmarks therefore need a degree of careful interpretation, and, if the focus of study is on the Roman period alone, evidence of this has to be identified, its traces filtered out from any earlier or later material and the true nature and extent of the Roman site revealed. Some types of site are distinctively of the Roman period. The 'playing-card' shape of the Roman fort or marching camp, the concentric Romano-Celtic temple, the sprawling plan of a villa and its associated barns and field systems. Not all, however, are easily assignable to any particular date, and in any compilation of aerial photographs many may comprise views of complex patterns of ditches and enclosures of uncertain date and function. The danger of assuming that even the most regular-looking of these is a Roman fort or fortlet was shown by one, at Appersley Dene in northern England, which lay neatly in association with a Roman road. For many years it was thought to be a fortlet, but on excavation it was found to be a small Roman or Iron Age farmstead surrounded by a ditch.

It is important to ensure that flying to record cropmark sites is co-ordinated and disciplined in the same way as any other form of research, or many hours will be spent in relatively fruitless repetition of the same pieces of work. Ideally, sites discovered will be indexed and plotted to a nationally agreed standard, known sites subjected to a comprehensive campaign of repeat visits at various times of the year and in various light conditions in order to extract the maximum possible information from them. Individual operators will be kept informed of other people's discoveries so that a research campaign can be built round them to augment and supplement known finds. Clearly this cannot realistically concentrate on the Roman period alone, and any interpretation of aerial photographs will have to take account of the palimpsest of the present-day landscape, in the same way that excavators who wish to reach Roman layers on an excavation have to progress to them through the remains of all subsequent periods.

Aerial photography has further drawbacks. One of the most obvious is that, apart from in those cases where the cropmark or earthwork is distinctive, sites can rarely be dated from the air. Unless the discovery of a site is followed by field-walking to gather artifacts from the ploughsoil and to find some firmer clue as to the context and date of the underlying features, mistakes and mis-attributions can be made. Even where an area can be studied comprehensively in this way, there is no guarantee that a site which shows up well as a cropmark will automatically produce diagnostic pottery or other artifacts in the ploughsoil above it, sufficient to enable a firm interpretation to be made.

Finally, there will always be areas of the landscape which for one reason or another are not conducive to the study of cropmarks. In some cases, post-Roman land-use may have totally obliterated or hidden any earlier material; in others, the underlying soil conditions are not favourable to showing the variations in crop growth which enable sites to be clearly pinpointed. On many distribution maps of sites, therefore, there will be a bias in favour of those areas where cropmarks can be seen, and this may cause problems for the comparison of Roman settlement patterns, e.g. in different areas of the countryside, on a variety of soil-types, or at varying contours. Apparent gaps in the record may also be the result of a lack of people actually carrying out flying, searching, and observation and its subsequent field-walking; it could be claimed with some justification, for example, that the apparent concentration of Roman villa sites in the Somme basin in France is almost entirely due to many years of flying and photography carried out by one individual. In other areas of Gaul, information about Roman villas comes from earlier field archaeology alone. There is no clear indication that the Somme basin was especially favoured by the Roman farmer, merely that our recovery of information about the period and the Roman use of the landscape is patchy.

When the presence of a site has been discovered from the air, it is important that as much as possible is learnt about it, and, for the purposes of research or protection of its remains, that its nature is determined as far as is possible. Many countries have an established antiquities service at either local or national level, which can gather information about sites, plot them accurately onto maps, and plan campaigns of research and investigation into them. Before excavation takes place, antiquarian accounts of finds in the neighbourhood should be investigated, or the fields should be walked (with the owner's permission) after ploughing in order to recover scattered pottery and artifacts and to record the relative distribution of surface finds. By this latter means, it is sometimes possible to pinpoint areas of particular interest within a large site, or to show areas where the agricultural regime may be causing damage to relatively undisturbed buried layers and features. In some cases, the ploughing regime on a site may be relatively stable, affecting only the topsoil layers which are churned over year after year. In others, the discovery of concentrations of quality finds, freshly broken pottery sherds, which clearly have not been continually abraded by many years of ploughing, may show that there is cause for concern, and that the site is suffering from the present regime.

The main tools for this kind of checking are the eyes and experience of archaeologists used to interpreting man's impact on his landscape, and spotting objects of interest and significance in the soil. There are mechanical aids, however, to the prospection of sites and to the location of finds within the soil. The most readily available is the metal detector, widely available in many countries, and sold as a machine which will enable the user to locate 'buried treasure'. Depending on the power of the machine, such detectors can pinpoint the presence of metal objects to a depth of more than a foot in the soil; they may tempt irresponsible operators to work over a site and dig holes to pluck potentially valuable finds – coins or metallic objects – from their context in the soil. The attraction of rifling archaeological sites in this way for private profit or to enhance personal collections of antiquities has proved too tempting for some operators. In some countries the use of these machines on protected sites is illegal or subject to strict controls, and the law is strictly applied. However, use of the machines within the context of a more professional examination of a site has on occasion formed a most useful adjunct to archaeological excavation or field-walking. On excavation they can accurately pinpoint the presence of buried metal objects and enable excavators not to miss coins, for example, whose existence they can mark for reference, and extract them from the ground as and when the relevant layers are reached and examined. In field-walking, metal detectors have been used like a pair of X-ray eyes, to scan a known ploughed site, and to locate and extract according to a grid system relevant finds from the already disturbed ploughsoil.

Sites can also be prospected by other, more sophisticated means. Geophysical surveys undertaken by magnetometer can cover large areas of a site relatively speedily. This kind of survey picks up traces of anything in the ground which bears a magnetic imprint – mainly burnt clay or hearths or iron objects. Buried walls will give a mild negative signal, and pits or ditches a mild positive one, compared to the background average of the site which is formed by the subsoil conditions. Resistivity surveying, on the other hand, is a process whereby an electric current is passed through ground marked out on a grid system between pairs of electrodes. The electric current passes easily through the softer, damper fill of pits and ditches, and sets up negative resistance, while the presence of compacted material, such as a buried wall, shows up as positive. This process, however, involving the careful gridding of a site, and the insertion of the pair of electrical probes to a constant depth, is labour-intensive, and has to be applied sparingly.

All these forms of analysis and prospection – the scrutiny of ancient sources and place-name evidence, the search through antiquarian records or museum collections, and the examination of sites from the air and subsequent verification on the ground – are essential precursors of a fuller archaeological exploration through excavation. They cannot hope to provide anything like the amount of detailed information which can be extracted from the site on excavation, but such is the cost of the labour-intensive effort of excavation that non-destructive surveys, field work, and research on the archaeological landscape are among the most important and cost-effective ways of learning more about the Roman period. The majority of known sites will not be subjected to comprehensive excavation; yet the planning of an excavation strategy for those which are examined may rely very heavily on information gained from other sites by just those methods described above.

It is not my purpose in this book to describe in detail the mechanics of excavation technique or the principles of stratification. The examination of a site by excavation is a specialized task which relies on keen observation, a disciplined and informed approach, meticulous recording of what is found, and accuracy and professionalism of planning, surveying, and photography. The exercise is unrepeatable: the techniques of carrying the job out must be equal to the task. But it is not sufficient to plan, plot, and identify each feature as it is uncovered. The whole strategy of excavation of a site depends in large measure upon the interpretation put upon it by the excavator as the work is in progress.

This is perhaps most easily illustrated by the following account of the excavation of an imaginary barrack block within a Roman fort occupied from AD80 until the end of the fourth century. Working backwards through the superimposed layers of buildings and occupation, attempting always to record and then remove each of the phases of buildings and associated features in reverse order, its excavator will first encounter the debris of demolition or collapse of the late Roman barrack blocks, perhaps unexpectedly irregular in plan. As these are examined and removed, with their associated rubbish pits, post-holes for lean-to sheds, and makeshift roofs, the plan may become a little more regular, and a barrack of more familiar plan, with a series of small rooms at one end and a centurion's quarters at the other, starts to appear. This has associated floor-levels, pits, and ovens, and may itself have been replanned several times, with partition walls added to the basic plan to afford specialized accommodation for different garrisons. Beneath this stone building and partly obscured by it lie the traces of at least two earlier phases of timber barrack blocks, on a different alignment, deliberately dismantled to enable their stone-built successors to occupy the same site. All that survives of them are the narrow, filled-in trenches which once contained sleeper-beams into which posts were inserted; these are filled with soil of a sharply different colour from the surrounding natural earth. Two distinct building plans, much mutilated by all the later stone buildings and pits dug on the site, can be identified. In addition, it can be seen that the colour of the soil filling one set of sleeper-beam trenches is black, suggesting that the trenches have been filled with a charcoal deposit after the destruction of the building by fire. It is clear that the trenches filled with this deposit, where they coincide with the other beam trenches, run through uninterrupted. It was thus the second phase of timber buildings which was destroyed by fire.

This hypothetical account, a simplified version of the sorts of evidence revealed by excavation, can only be the product of a series of interpretations and judgements such as are inherent in any excavation campaign. Objectives which an archaeologist will always have to bear in mind are to interpret what is found, to assign it to its correct phase and context, and to sort out its relationship to other layers. On a large site, one would normally expect to see the whole area excavated at the same pace. It would be unnecessarily complicated, for example, to excavate down to the timber phases of the barrack at one end, while the other end was still at its stone period destruction levels. The excavator must keep a running check, as far as possible, on the artifacts coming out of the occupation layers, pits, and post-holes, attempting always to determine from the types of pottery and small finds emerging what date the features currently under excavation belong to.

Before getting to the stage of undertaking an excavation, however, a number of other considerations should have passed through the excavator's mind. These are part of the whole strategy of examination of the site. First, what has been discovered from earlier excavations – what degree of disruption, or what depth of topsoil or Roman deposits can be expected? Has the site been subjected to ploughing in the immediate post-Roman, medieval, or relatively modern past? If so, what effect might this have had on the remains? Or has there been some other structure on the site which may have caused later damage – a farmstead or barn, for example, whose remains may confuse the picture revealed by the excavation?

Questions of a more strategic nature ought also to be considered: what is the overall aim of the excavation, apart from the examination of this one barrack area of the site? The information gained will reveal the detail only about the specific site under examination; but it may have a more general application to other sites. A research plan which aims at formulating and answering more general questions about this type of site should therefore always be borne in mind. To what extent do the changes in plan of the barracks reflect a change in use of the buildings, alterations in the fort garrison, or changing numbers of troops in garrison at the fort? Consideration should be given to ways of gathering information whilst the excavation is in progress which can help towards answering these sorts of questions, which need to be formulated before the start of the work. To provide data relevant to these specific problems, it may be productive to decide to plot the find-spot of each artifact recovered from the barrack in order to enable more detailed study to take place at a later stage into the potentially diverse uses of the building at different dates. In addition, by recording the find-spot of every element of building material recovered, it may be possible to make provision for the eventual examination of types of nails, tiles, and other building supplies in an attempt to distinguish variations in materials and constructional techniques which might have been the result of work by different troop units.

There will always be limitations to the amount of interpretation any site and its finds can legitimately support, and in many cases where we wish to know more it may be that the archaeological data will never give the required precision for firm conclusions to be drawn. If archaeologists tackle the task of excavating the site without having considered the sorts of questions they wish to attempt to answer, and without formulating their excavation strategy in a way which will improve their chances of doing so, progress and significant gains in knowledge will be all the more fortuitous. This is not to say that an archaeologist should be blinkered whilst excavation is in progress: the unexpected is always liable to appear, and has to be met, and strategies have to be adopted to deal with it which may even run counter to the original research design. Within the framework of clear and objective gathering of information about a site, there has to be scope both for a response to what is actually discovered and for interpretation of the significance of the finds. All this forms the service supplied by the excavator.

A service, however, is normally performed for a client, and the archaeologist performs within a professional discipline comparable in many ways to that of the architect or of the surveyor. On one level, the archaeologist is recording, measuring, and planning remains of ancient buildings, using techniques which are not dissimilar to those used in other professions. On another level, he is expected to bring a high degree of understanding about what he finds to bear on the remains, to be able to interpret what is being found, and to develop his campaign of examination in response to continuing discoveries. At the same time, he is undertaking what has been described as the 'unrepeatable experiment'. Unlike the architect, however, the archaeologist has no obvious single 'client' at whose behest the work is undertaken and whose requirements are met and whose instructions are followed throughout the performance of this professional service.

In many countries there are public bodies – museums, government departments, or research institutes, under a variety of names and titles – who take on the task of planning and funding archaeological work, whether as part of a research or a survey programme. These may be seen as a measure of the importance that each particular country attaches to the discovery and examination of information about its past. Perhaps the clearest indicator of the extent of any country's recognition of the importance of its past is the extent to which funding is made available to preserve buildings, and to record, manage, or excavate archaeological sites liable to be affected or damaged as a result of development or other pressures of land-use. Thus, in practice, the main client for archaeological work tends to be the 'heritage' body of each country: responsibility thus falls on those who keep the public purse to apply funds on archaeological work to their best advantage.

At the same time, other bodies, groups, or scholars may wish to engage in research excavation. These may be as diverse as a research department of a university, a local group of enthusiasts, and an owner of a site who wishes to see it developed for its tourist potential. Their accountability is to others whose interests in the sites they are dealing with are commensurate with their own, to those in both the present and the future who will cast a critical eye over what they are doing, and to the rest of the archaeological world and to the public at large for their handling of this small portion of the finite resource of archaeological sites. If the study of Roman archaeology is to progress and develop, high standards of practice and interpretation must be expected of amateur and professional alike. This requires funding, support services, planning and publication of results, for which any amount of enthusiasm, though always welcome, is no substitute.

7

The study of artifacts

Roman sites in general produce an abundance of finds, particularly pottery, glass, and metalware. Many a museum show-case is crammed with distinctive Roman pottery or metalwork, and the task of showing enough to stimulate visitors' interest without losing the balance within the collections on display a difficult one. Deep in museum basements, there will often be row upon row of boxes containing Roman finds, far too much to put on permanent view, an eloquent testimony to the plentiful finds of this date, and a considerable storage problem for museum staff.

Seeing and handling such material has an immediacy; it establishes contact with the Roman men and women who also touched and used it. The craftsmanship can still be seen and appreciated, and the nature of the evidence it presents is direct. These objects reflect contemporary tastes and preferences, and can carry an unconscious message about the people of Rome and its empire.

Although a number of museum finds are works of art from antiquity collected mainly during the course of the eighteenth and nineteenth centuries by travellers and connoisseurs, most of the material stored in present-day museum collections will have a recorded provenance, and is likely to be the product of the excavation of a particular site. To know where material was originally found is of great importance; several classes of finds exhibit a strong regional identity within the Roman world, and to know for certain that material can be assigned to a particular find-spot helps to set it in context, and enables comparison with related discoveries. The major benefit, however, comes from the study of finds from within an excavated site. Here, arguments work in two directions: analysis of finds from a site can help interpret, understand, and date it; or the form and function of a site can give meaning to material found there and enable other sites with similar material to be better interpreted.

Portable finds represent the whole gamut of material from everyday life, both common and unusual. Space would not allow a full catalogue, but it would include personal items: clothing and jewellery, statues, ornaments, toys and models; materials used in the home: pottery, glassware, and lamps; tools and equipment of many types; weapons and uniforms. The majority of the material which survives is of what we would regard as non-perishable material; thus, while finds of ceramics, glass, metal, and bone material are relatively commonplace, there are far fewer organic remains such as textiles, leather, wood, or foodstuffs, though even these can survive where conditions (usually waterlogged or otherwise airless) allow.

￼ Functions of most objects are obvious – many, as in the case of woodworking tools or surgical instruments, can readily be deduced from objects of essentially similar design in use today or in the recent past. Others, like the 'dodecahedra', baffle expert and layman alike, though normally these afford ample scope and little discouragement for imaginative and scholarly speculation about an object's original use. All classes of material attract the attention of individual experts and specialists whose detailed knowledge of the subject based on the classification of site finds, their relationship to and comparison with others of the same type, and resulting attempts at suggesting dates when they may have been in use, are all very important and useful to the archaeologist.

Paradoxically, it is not necessarily from the most spectacular finds that the archaeologist can hope to extract the maximum amount of useful information. A hoard of gold and silver tableware may tell us a great deal about its find-spot, prompt speculation about the lifestyle of its Roman owners, or lead to theories about why the valuables may have been lost or buried; but, because of its rarity, it will not normally provide material which can be easily compared with other finds from nearby. More helpful are finds which have a good survival rate, are more or less imperishable, and are commonly encountered on many different sites. Analysis of these can help establish links and distribution patterns. If, in addition, this material also appears in a series of standard shapes and sizes, this will legitimately allow correlation and comparison to be drawn between finds from different sites. Several classes of material from the ancient world fulfil some or all of these criteria. Some forms of metalwork are found in standardized shapes and sizes, particularly when supplied for the use of the Roman army. Glassware comes in certain regular shapes and sizes, though it is not as common as other materials, nor so easily recoverable. Site-finds which most readily furnish material for analysis in all these ways by the archaeologist, however, are coins and pottery, and, since Roman pottery represents easily the bulk of finds from most sites, it is the material which has seen most concentrated study.

￼ The process of building up a picture of the past through the study of Roman pottery relies on the examination of the material itself and of its find-spot, particularly if this is in a well-documented, fully excavated site. The excavator will have patiently examined all the layers and levels encountered there; the ditches and pits will probably have been emptied while all the superimposed floor and make-up levels associated with buildings will have been examined in detail. All the finds will have been washed or cleaned, marked or labelled (to show where they came from), and prepared for examination at a later date. The excavator will naturally enough be keen to use all the excavated material, including the pottery, to give a closer dated framework for the structural developments recorded at the site: pottery here plays an important, but not exclusive, role. Before it is used for the purposes of applying a series of dates to the site, its distribution within the site has often to be rather better understood, for this can help reveal aspects about the site which will assist in interpreting it.

First, forms of pottery found at various points on the site may indicate what those areas were being used for. Distinctive material – crucibles, cooking pots, or wine vats – taken together with other evidence, may betray the presence of a smithy, a kitchen, a bar, or a storage area. Groups of pottery may also be found concentrated in one place, perhaps in a potter's shop or workshop; if a deposit of pottery of this nature can be identified with certainty, it will not only help to interpret the function of that part of the site, but will assist in working out a date for the vessels themselves. A group of pottery awaiting sale on the shelves of a store may contain examples of all sorts and shapes of vessels; if one can make some estimate for 'shelf-life', the pottery can be presumed to have been in contemporary or near-contemporary use.

Second, it may be possible from the shapes or styles of some of the pots to say what they were used for. There are dangers in this; pottery containers, sometimes distinctive, sometimes not, can be used for a multitude of purposes – feeding bottles, chamber pots, honey jars, money boxes, paint pots, oil lamps – and it is by no means certain that Roman forms of these items would necessarily be paralleled by what might be regarded as standard modern-day examples. Association of pottery with other artifacts may give further clues to its use, if for example a residue of paint is found in the base of a jar, or if a vessel is used as a burial urn or as a container for a coin-hoard.

Third, and possibly even more difficult, it may be possible to gauge standards of living at a site under examination from the types and styles of pottery discovered there. Archaeologists tend to group Roman pottery into either 'fine' or 'coarse' wares. Within the former classification come well-finished, glazed, or decorated wares such as *terra nigra* or *terra sigillata*; within the latter, such material as plain grey-ware cooking pots and jars which might be products of a local kiln. There are, however, many gradations of fineness and coarseness between these two extremes, and, in any case, our modern judgement of values which labels one pot fine and another coarse may not have been shared by their Roman owners or users. After all, much of the *sigillata* produced in Gaul was supplied to the army on campaign and on the imperial frontiers. Clearly the considerable quantities of this type of red-glazed decorated or plain

110

ware found on Roman fort sites cannot be realistically regarded as the equivalent of the regimental silver, and it is obvious that this sort of pottery was in everyday use in mess and barrack rooms. Should we thus consider it 'fine' ware other than in terms of its excellent finish?

— Some initial assessment of the type of site under investigation can perhaps be gained from the comparative proportions of 'fine' and 'coarse' wares found there, the range of pottery types which came from other than the local region, and the decorative quality of the painted or figured wares. This will be to some extent a subjective view, only offset, if it can be done, by comparing material from this site with types of pottery found on other sites in the same region. If the material found here stands out as of a completely different character and mix, then conclusions about the wealth of the owners, the importance of the site, and the possible extent of its influence can be considered.

— The excavator must also consider the context in which material from the site is found today. Much of it may come from pits or ditches which have become filled with rubbish; it may have been deliberately discarded or accidentally lost. Other finds, as is often the case in campaign forts of the first century, may be discovered in considerable quantities in filled up trenches left after the extraction of the foundation sleeper-beams or upright posts of wooden buildings. Here, the freshness of the breaks in the pottery, or the recovery, albeit in pieces, of entire or near-complete vessels, can suggest that it was deliberately smashed to render it useless, and deposited in any convenient pit within a fort as it was being abandoned in favour of a new site elsewhere. In other cases still, the build-up of layers of occupation within a building, or perhaps beneath its suspended timber floors, may be a very good indicator of the length and intensity of the building's use. Some assessment of the reason for the deposition of the finds must always be attempted, or there will be a danger of seeing them merely as something conveniently left behind by the Romans to help us assess their date or lifestyle. What the archaeologist studies, however, is by and large what the Romans discarded or what, once lost, did not seem worth retrieving. The places in which rubbish was deposited, or the reasons why lost material was not reclaimed, may on occasion be as significant or informative as the material itself.

— Consideration of the dating properties of pottery has deliberately been left to the last in order to draw attention to these other forms of information which can come from site-finds and which may have a bearing on the dating eventually assigned to it. One is more likely to date pottery from a building or from the fill of a ditch accurately if the history of how and why the pottery was deposited there in the first place can be understood. In addition, before assigning a date to the site on the basis of material recovered from it, some estimate of the length of time that, for example, a pot had been in use at the site before being dumped or lost where the archaeologist finds it has to be attempted, and any such estimate may depend on the value or the function of the pot. A clear distinction has to be drawn between the date of manufacture of pottery and the date when it was finally deposited in the ground.

If we suppose, however, that the ceramic material from the site under study has no established framework for a dated sequence, the archaeologist will have to organize it so that it can be of maximum use for the interpretation of the site. First, the archaeologist will want to look hard at the sequence of layers and levels which come from the site itself. Here the rules of stratigraphy – observation about which features on the site follow or cut through others – will give an outline sequence. This in turn will lead to a series of phase plans showing changes over the whole site at each particular stage in the site's development. Thus, related and near-contemporary pits, ditches, foundation trenches, and occupation levels, all of which may contain pottery and other artifacts, can be identified. When the pottery from these linked deposits is studied, therefore, it is being looked at more or less in the correct sequence of its deposition in the soil.

The pottery from the site can then be sorted into types and fabrics, looking first at the shapes, colours, and sizes of the vessels and their decoration, and then in more detail at the clays from which the pots are made, by examining their colours, their particle size, and the types of inclusions or tempering materials in the fabric. At a first sort, many different fabrics and types may be identified; further work and comparison may begin to reduce the numbers of separate categories of pottery, e.g. by revealing that pots of completely different shape are made from the same clays, and can therefore be identified as products of the same group of kilns. This sort of classification of pottery from a site is a painstaking business, but if solid conclusions are to be drawn from the work in the end, it is important that accurate observations are made and that the assessment of the material in terms of its shape, colour, fabric, and 'feel' is as objective as possible.

The material having been classified into a series of types, an attempt to form a view of the pottery as a whole can begin. The material can be analysed in terms of the comparative frequency of various forms or fabrics of pottery within the sequence of layers and deposits. By doing this, a relative chronology of the pottery can be built up: certain types will appear in the earliest layers, and will be found in later ones only as small abraded fragments, if at all. Others will not be found in the early layers, but will suddenly begin to be common at a later stage, gradually increasing in proportion to other fabrics, and then perhaps dying away. Others still may be represented only at one particular phase in the use of the site. When compared in this way, the various types of pottery can normally be assigned a chronological 'frequency curve' which covers their introduction, main period of use, and decline. At this stage, it is sufficient to set the pottery in its relationship to other fabrics and wares in this way, without attempting to assign dates to the vessels. In fact, what is here being dated is not so much the pottery itself as the periods at which it was deposited in the ground, though this cannot fail to be related in some measure to its overall availability.

Fortunately, most archaeological deposits contain other material – metalwork, glassware, and coins – which can be classified in the same sorts of ways, though because such finds are rather rarer they seldom afford such a comprehensive assemblage of relevant material for study. In any search for close dating, it is clear that coins are of great importance, for they normally bear a date of minting. The association of pottery with these or with others artifacts – glassware, brooches, or belt-buckles – which themselves may have been distinctive or fashionable at particular times, can be of benefit for arriving at firm dates or for comparing groups or deposits of material from one site with others on sites nearby. If in addition there is reason to believe from its military origin or from consideration of its distribution or marketing patterns that this material is from a common supplier, this kind of comparison can act as an aid to an understanding of the correct chronological relationship between different sorts of pottery wares and other artifacts which will apply to the whole of a local area.

In all these ways, an outline relative chronology can be established for the site and by inference for the finds from it, but this does not necessarily produce any clues as to its absolute date. Certain links can be made: it is immediately obvious that a pit, for example, cannot have been filled until after the date of manufacture of the latest object found buried within it. Thus, if dates of manufacture can be attached to artifacts, at least a date can be established after which the various pits and ditches, occupation levels and trenches on the site being examined were filled with the material they now contain.

Apart from the obvious medium of coins, already mentioned, there is one other form of Roman find which has long been recognized as of great usefulness and importance for this form of study. One of the commonest forms of pottery, virtually empire-wide, since it was produced for and used by the Roman army, is the distinctive orange-red *terra sigillata*. Work on this material since the later years of the last century has concentrated on the classification of various standard forms in which it was made, the identification of its production centres, and, because many of the vessels are stamped with potters' names, or bear figured decoration, on the products of individual potters recognizable from their styles of workmanship.

In very simple terms, the main results of all this work are the

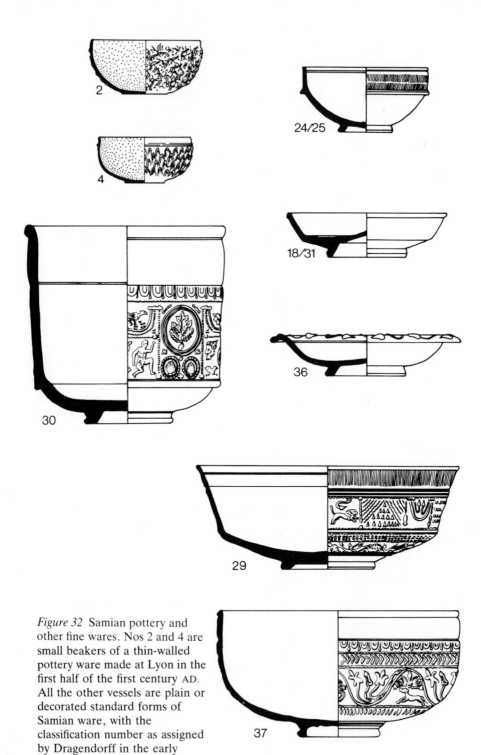

Figure 32 Samian pottery and other fine wares. Nos 2 and 4 are small beakers of a thin-walled pottery ware made at Lyon in the first half of the first century AD. All the other vessels are plain or decorated standard forms of Samian ware, with the classification number as assigned by Dragendorff in the early twentieth century

conclusions that these wares were produced in three centres, in southern, central, and eastern Gaul, apparently from the early years of the first century AD until about the mid third century. Because the work of so many individual potters can be recognized, a mere fragment of a bowl bearing a figured scene or part of one of the name-stamps can usually be assigned to a known potter. This of course limits the period at which the vessel could have been produced to the lifetime of this particular individual. In addition, it is clear from site-finds and from other well-dated examples that production in the kilns concentrated on a different range of shapes at different periods, even though there are some vessel forms which seem to have been made throughout the life of the industry.

Armed with all this information about production centres, potters, and vessel forms, not only from *terra sigillata* but from other industries whose products have been equally well studied, it is necessary now to go back to the finds from individual sites in order to attempt a closer dating. Some finds have been spectacular and significant enough to enable clear links to be established between material found on site and dated historical events. In 1881, in the ruins of Pompeii, a consignment of thirty-seven pottery lamps from North Italy, together with eighty-seven *terra sigillata* bowls of two common shapes, but by a number of different potters, were found still packed in the crate in which they had been delivered. This stock of pottery and lamps can only have arrived in Pompeii shortly before the disaster which befell it in AD79. Thus this material, by the potters Mommo, Vitalis, and others from southern Gaul, can be assigned precise date of deposition, and, by implication, since they had just arrived crated from the factory, of manufacture. Further study of such wares took place around the turn of this century on finds from the frontier zones in Germany, where identification and exploration revealed sites of forts which belonged to phases of Roman military expansion in the area. Historical sources record that this phase of military absorption was taking place during the first century, and therefore material found at these sites could be assigned dates linked to a relatively assured historical and chronological framework.

There is a need for continual assessment and refinement of dating derived by historically related material such as this. There are always dangers that arguments deployed to date either the sites or the pottery from them may become circular and self-justificatory. It is difficult to be certain at times whether the site dates the pottery or the pottery the site. Ideally, to keep estimates of the dates of various vessel forms and types under revision, there needs to be a marriage of two forms of information: from the production centres come details about the potters, their artistic styles, and their preferred vessel shapes, while from the sites come a series of interlinked, ordered, chronological relationships. Any resulting attempt to assign dates must be a balance between accepting the

Figure 33 Three of the Samian ware bowls from Pompeii discovered still packed in their crates at the time of the eruption of Vesuvius: (a) Form 29, by the potter Vitalis (active AD60–85); (b) Form 29 by the potter Mommo; (c) Form 37 by Mommo

traditional historically derived date for the material, and applying this rigidly to date everything else, and the opposite extreme, the rather perverse refusal to consider any 'accepted' date for ceramic material on the grounds that it may unduly begin to influence one's view of the observed chronological sequence as recorded on site.

It remains true, however, that much of the dating of other Roman pottery wares, local or regional, relies to a large degree on a series of links and relationships as site finds with the comparatively easily datable forms of *terra sigillata*. Allowance must always be made for the length of time since its production that the pottery has been in use, for the distance from the point of manufacture that it has had to travel, and for the value which provincial Romans may have put upon it, and hence how carefully they may have used it. All this can make an assessment of the date of deposition of the material very difficult to determine. In a relatively recent study in the southern suburbs of Roman London, statistical analysis of the range of probability dating for pottery within a group of contexts produced a series of average ages for deposited *sigillata* ranging from 25 years between AD65 and 90, 30 years from AD90 to 130, and around 40 years between AD130 and 180. Adequate and accurate assessment of this type of factor is relatively rare, and is only possible where the ceramic material itself can be closely dated. In periods after the *sigillata* industry had closed down, there are hardly any examples of standardized empire-wide wares, and few historically attested events, like the destruction of Pompeii, which can help by providing agreed dated contexts for groups of ceramic material. Often, the archaeologist has to be content with a date no more precise than 'first half of the fourth century' for the production of later pottery. If one then has to allow that the material could have been deposited in the ground any time up to 40 or 50 years after its manufacture, it is clear that an archaeological context cannot, on this material alone, be assigned a date any more precise than within the correct century or so.

Most of this discussion so far has centred on Roman pottery, but coins are also commonly regarded by the archaeologist as of equal if not greater importance, particularly for the information they give about the dating of the site. This deserves more scrutiny, for ostensibly the Roman coin, which bears the mint-mark and the head of an emperor, can normally be dated to within a year or two. As a manufactured item, the coin is far more precisely datable than any other artifact.

Like pottery, coins need to be studied in their own right as artifacts and as tokens in order to appreciate their significance as site-finds. Ordering the specimens in a typological series, working out the sequence of mint-marks, recognizing individual die-stamps, and ascertaining the order of their use, is the work of the professional numismatist. On the basis of the typological series of the coins from any given reign, it may be possible to draw historical conclusions from the often propagandist messages which the coins bear, to view the quality of the coinage as an indicator of the economic background of the times, or to assess the ways in which different Roman emperors and their administrations attempted to use their coinage and fiscal policies to balance the conflicting demands of trade, the armies, and their rivals for imperial power. Such work is specialized – the numismatist's equivalent to the close study of potters and fabrics of Samian ware – which aims to study coins to a large degree independently of their contexts, and to glean the maximum of information from them as historical documents in their own right.

The archaeologist who has excavated a site, however, is often on the lookout for something a little more specific. They will know that the date of minting, which can be read within the legend borne by the coin deposited in a pit, gives a definable historical date after which that pit must have been filled up. Overall, too, the span of dates provided by coin-finds from the site will doubtless cover a considerable period; many will have come from securely defined levels and layers, but others will have come from topsoil layers and levels already disturbed before the excavation took place. What more can be said about the site from the coins it has produced?

The first thing to note is that although most pottery is broken or metalwork damaged when cast aside, coins never totally lose their usefulness, though they can sometimes become substantially debased or devalued. Coins found during excavation, therefore, were probably lost and not sought rather than deliberately buried or thrown out (like other 'rubbish'), and those found today probably represent what the site's inhabitants could best afford to lose. For this reason, it is probable that the total amount of coinage represented by finds on site to study and draw conclusions from is only a minute proportion of the total numbers of coins actually circulating in the Roman period. It has been suggested, for example, that for some sites, the amount of coin represented in our coin-lists is no more than 0.1 per cent of what would have been in circulation in the Roman period, and even then formed only by the small change, the least valuable currency.

There is a value in looking at coin-finds, not only on those sites where a spread of coins has been found within a well-documented and extended period of occupation, but also at sites where a substantial number of chance finds of Roman coins have been made over a long period of time. Coin-lists from such places are likely to be more representative of the total numbers of coins in circulation throughout the Roman period. By analysing finds from sites such as these, phase by phase, it is possible to determine those occasions in the Roman period when coins were in common circulation and when they were rarer – perhaps respectively at times when there was high inflation and small change was worth very little, or when the commonest coins were valuable and people accepted their loss only with reluctance and after a great deal of searching. If, province by province, this sort of work is done on coin-lists from major Roman centres, a general picture of the coinage in circulation is built up. Site-finds can be measured against this to see if there are any local anomalies. If there are, historical or economic conclusions about activity at the site can possibly be drawn, though much will depend on the size of the sample under discussion. It is already becoming clear, however, that in certain cases military sites have a different pattern of coin-loss from sites which are predominantly civilian, and the extent to which coins from a site under study fall into either a 'civilian' or a 'military' pattern (always assuming that these can be defined) could show the extent of commercial or military pressures on its development.

The conclusion that if no coins are found there was no activity on the site is not necessarily tenable. The archaeologist must appreciate that the coins found on site are the product of a combination of factors which must be understood as a whole. Individual coins are still of use, provided that some assessment can be made of the length of time they had been in circulation. Because of the intrinsic value of coins, this is always harder to determine than in the case of pottery. Some indication can be gained from the degree of wear to which a coin has been exposed, but this is not conclusive, for freshly minted or undamaged coins tend to be retained as savings, and thus could be as long-lived as a coin which is heavily worn.

There is one further class of coinage which merits at least a mention. Coin-hoards are a relatively frequent, often chance find whose interpretation occasions considerable difficulties. Modern analysis seeks to define two different types of hoard, one composed of currency – a cross-section of the coin available at the time – the other of savings, containing mainly unworn coins perhaps set aside over a longish period. There is a temptation to argue further that hoards were deposited quite soon after the date of the latest coin within them. When their find-spots are plotted on maps according to the date of the latest coin they contain, and compared with historical sources speaking of unrest or invasion, they have been claimed to show deposits of savings or valuables sparked off by the onset of unease caused by a marauding band or the movement of an invading people.

Such easy conclusions as these are dangerous. We do not necessarily know why coins which are today recovered as hoards were buried in the first place, nor, except in particular circumstances, where there is a large amount of closely contemporary-looking material within a restricted area, can many valid conclusions be drawn. Finally, those hoards which are available today for study are actually those which failed – their owners never reclaimed them. It would be easy to give an overblown historical interpretation of this fact, and claim in graphic terms that their erstwhile

119

owners must have been overtaken by an awful calamity: the truth is, of course, that there may be a number of individual reasons for the owners' failure to recover their buried savings, ranging from accident or wilfulness to sheer forgetfulness. The archaeologist treads in this psychological minefield at his peril.

As well as providing the basis for all aspects of site interpretation discussed so far, finds such as pottery and glassware can also be used and assessed in different ways. First, the study of the material can lead to the identification of areas of production; on occasion, scientific techniques of examining pottery clays may identify the source of raw materials and may show that pottery with differing surface finishes (sometimes glazed or slipped, sometimes reduced) are products of the same industry. Once the existence of an industry has been identified with certainty, products from the factories can be identified in assemblages of finds from sites both nearby and further afield.

This in turn enables study of distribution patterns from the production site to be undertaken. Where the industry is comparatively localized, this can be of significance in determining market patterns, the range of distribution by road or by river, and the relative distribution patterns of different pottery wares, and hence estimates of the relative value and desirability of the products of rival kilns seeking to supply the same market. Certain trends may suggest themselves in explanation of the observed facts. In one example, 'finer' wares can be shown to have a wider market penetration from a distribution centre in those areas served by main roads; the higher production cost (and the assumed consequent higher price to the consumer) of the better finished wares is offset by the ease of distribution along the main communications networks and makes these better-quality wares a strong market competitor against less well-finished, cheaper material. Once off the main highways, however, the distribution of the finer vessels tails off in favour of the plainer wares; this suggests that the cheaper price of the plain wares made them competitive where transport costs added significantly to the price.

Empire-wide distribution patterns can also be studied, and the main arteries of cross-provincial trade identified, from the discovery of pottery and other distinctive material on both sides of a natural barrier such as the English Channel. Considerable amounts of first- to third-century pottery from Gaul and the Rhineland are known in Britain, but the extent of the trade interchange both ways across the channel in the late third and the fourth centuries is only now being discovered. British pottery from the Oxfordshire and New Forest industries has been identified in coastal regions of northern Gaul, while products from Argonne, the Tours region of Gaul, and the Eifel have now been recorded on British sites.

Such signs as these, restricted to pottery, are arguably only one indicator of a much larger trade in perishables of all sorts which flourished in the ancient world. Foodstuffs of many kinds – figs, lentils, cucumbers, spices, and olive oil – will have flowed into British channel ports, while in the other direction went skins, woollen fabrics, hunting dogs, corn, and probably beer. The major trades which can still be identified tend to be those which used a distinctive container for their wares, such as the Mediterranean-based trade in garum, or salt-fish. But by far the most distinctive is the amphora, carrying wine or oil of many kinds around the empire. The extent of this trade in antiquity can be judged from the sheer size, at fifty metres high, of Monte Testaccio, near the warehouse quarter of Rome on the Tiber's edge. The whole hill is formed of broken fragments of amphorae thrown out from boats moored at the wharves. The deposits seem to have grown up over about 150 years within the first two centuries AD.

Further indications of the ubiquity of trade in the Mediterranean can be seen in the numbers of wrecked ships of Roman date. Upwards of 200 wrecks of the Roman imperial period are known, mainly within the western portion of the Mediterranean. While the significance of the distribution patterns of such wrecks is difficult to determine, their concentration round Spain in the first and second centuries AD perhaps reflects the importance of the Spanish wine trade at this time. A cluster of wrecks around Sicily and Sardinia dating slightly later suggests that trade with Africa may have increased in importance. In addition to their significance for understanding ancient trading patterns, such finds as these enable techniques of Roman ship-building and carpentry to be studied in detail, as well as providing further groups of artifacts, wooden or otherwise perishable, which would not normally survive on land.

— Wrecks are increasingly revealing how sizeable individual Roman merchant shipping could be – some have been estimated from their remains to be up to 600 tons in size. Trade was well organized and diverse; many of the vessels were laden with varied cargoes. While some ships carried supplies of quarried marble or ingots of raw material, the main bulk of cargoes was amphorae for oil, wine, or other perishable produce in considerable numbers; one wreck, dated to the first century BC, lying at Madragues de Giens, off the French coast near Toulon, contained about 7,000 amphorae, stacked in three or four layers. These, together with black- and red-glazed pottery found in the same wreck, give the archaeologist as complete a contemporary and consistent group of pottery types as any found in use at the moment when Vesuvius overcame Pompeii in AD79. Other wrecks in the same general area had a more varied cargo: Dramont D, near the Rhône mouth, dating from the mid first century AD, contained a cargo of mortaria (mixing bowls) from Italy, Rhodian amphorae containing figs, and amphorae of Greek type, probably from Africa, containing dates. Identification of the contents of

Figure 34 The wreck at Madragues de Giens, near Toulon, France, showing the cargo of amphorae she was carrying when she sank in the mid-first century AD

these amphorae was possible from the remains of skins and seeds of the fruits found within them.

Dated groups such as these are of immense use, for the more such combinations of contemporary objects can be defined, the better we are able to give a framework to all the objects within the group, and begin to transfer the well-dated sequences which can be applied to *terra sigillata*, for example, to other wares and artifacts. The study of wrecks, however, has its own particular hazards, quite apart from the logistics of the necessary equipment and expertise: once sunk, a ship may not stay in one piece. If in shallow water, there is a good chance that it will break up, or, if it lies in a particularly dangerous spot, there is a likelihood that other ships will come to grief at different times in the same neighbourhood, making the definition of which scattered finds on the sea-bed belong to which vessel a difficult one. Nor can it be certain to what extent the known concentrations of wrecks of Roman or any other date in the Mediterranean are really representative of the volume of trade in those zones in antiquity rather than a product of increased present-day leisure and holiday activities on the Spanish, French, and Italian coasts, which have enabled scuba divers to scan the area much more closely than has happened, for example, along the coastlines of much of North Africa. The known wrecks of Roman date in the western Mediterranean are a sample, but are they fully representative of the volume or the direction of trade?

Further aids to the dating of pottery artifacts come from a pair of scientific techniques. Archaeomagnetism is a dating method which can be used on any fixed structure – a fireplace, hearth, or kiln – made of clay fired *in situ* and left undisturbed since. Its principle is that, on firing to a certain temperature, magnetically sensitive mineral particles in the clay lose their original magnetic orientation, and take up a new one parallel to that of the magnetic field of the earth as it prevailed at the time. As the earth's magnetic poles can be shown to have been constantly on the move during the course of the last 2,000 years at least, accurate measurement of the magnetic orientation of the kiln can be used to show in which direction magnetic north lay at the time of last firing. The date at which magnetic north lay in this direction is also the date of the kiln. Although fine in theory, this dating method is not wholly independent of archaeologically or historically derived dates, for to establish dated points for magnetic north, historically dated kilns have to be used. Thus although arguments can again become circular, the more refinements made to the sequence of attested readings for the positioning of magnetic north which fit in with the curve produced so far, the more reliable will be any dates assigned to otherwise undated sites.

This technique applies only to fixed structures, but some progress is possible in measuring the intensity of the magnetic imprint 'trapped' by a pot at the time of its firing. The earth's magnetic field has not been constant in strength, and if a comparative reading can be gained from the magnetic intensity of Roman pottery at various dates against a known constant, it is possible that pottery bearing the same intensity can be assigned to the same date of manufacture. Here, too, any dates produced by this method must be derived from readings from 'well-dated' pots, and there are few pots which can be assigned with certainty to production in a single year. Intensity of magnetism might vary, too, from region to region, so there is not necessarily any link between pottery produced in widely different areas of the Roman world.

The other dating technique applicable specifically to pottery is thermoluminescence. Minerals in the clays from which pottery or tile is made contain radioactivity which gradually decays, but part of which is stored in impurities in the mineral crystals. This radioactivity is released as tiny amounts of light when the clays are heated to firing temperature when the pot is made. After firing, the impurities once more start to soak up minuscule amounts of the stored radiation, in a steady process which will continue until the material is heated once more to the same sort of temperature. When subjected to these heats, the radiation is given off as light, which can be measured. In theory, the greater the amount of stored radiation recorded, the older the pot should be, but not all the radiation stored in the pot comes from its own internal decaying radiation isotopes: some is also collected from the surrounding soil or from the earth's natural radiation. Different clays, too, naturally contain different proportions of sensitive material. The equipment used for measuring has to be capable of extremely accurate measurement, and the samples of pottery used for the testing need to be very carefully prepared and themselves analysed to assess their natural radiation propensities so that the amount of thermoluminescence can be correctly calibrated. The technique has not yet become so accurate that dating of Roman pottery to within a few years is possible. It has, however, shown up one or two spectacular fakes – for example stamped 'Roman' tiles from the fourth-century site of Pevensey, on the southern coast of Britain, which purported to prove rebuilding at the site under the late fourth-century emperor Honorius, have been clearly shown by these methods to be spurious, and to date from the nineteenth century.

Roman military uniforms and equipment afford an example showing how many of the methods of study outlined in this chapter can be applied to the study of a corpus of material. The first problem is to define what actually counts, and what the Romans themselves would have considered as military equipment. We may be helped to recognize and identify belt and scabbard fittings, portions of body armour, or any of the individual elements of a Roman soldier's uniform from contemporary portrayals of Roman soldiers in armour as seen on tombstones, or on monuments like Trajan's Column. To supplement these, it will be necessary to examine material found at known or assumed Roman fort sites, to identify – perhaps only from twisted fragments – those items which appear to be specifically military in purpose. Weapons, which are relatively distinctive, or complete sets of armour are easily recognizable: the main problems of identification come with small, detached hinges or decorations, originally from body armour, leather belts, or scabbards. These, though perhaps equally distinctive and of military purpose, are not so easily recognized without first understanding what they once formed part of.

Once identified with certainty, distribution patterns, forms of stylistic decoration, or detailed analysis of the metallic composition of this material may begin to identify particular products, and, from a consideration of the areas where these are found, give clues as to the whereabouts of the production centres themselves. Although such patterns of distribution may give more information about the deployment of Roman troops than about production and marketing in antiquity, the area supplied by individual workshops can be defined from the find-spots of equipment bearing a marked decorative style, or composed of a distinctive chemical or metallic alloy. Alternatively, since historical sources and archaeological finds (for example tombstones or tile-stamps) forge a clear link between individual legions or units of auxiliary troops and the sites which must have been their permanent station, certain elements of military equipment, which are found to correspond in their patterns of distribution with the areas of influence of identifiable troop units, could pinpoint specific 'regimental' uniforms. This in turn would help to identify troops on the move round the Roman world by plotting all the locations where such material is found.

The process of understanding the material has, however, to dig rather deeper. Literary sources record that each Roman legion had its own body of craftsmen. Surviving contemporary papyri and writing tablets show that the normal run of unskilled soldiers' duties included being drafted into the fort workshops where, even in an auxiliary fort on the northern frontier of Britain, specialist craftsmen making shields and swords were at work. One of the tablets found in the pre-Hadrianic levels at Vindolanda gives a duty-roster for work in the *fabrica* which details work for 343 men, hinting that such duties were a major part of the troops' activities in peacetime, and that since not all of the men could be expected to be skilled, the majority were engaged on labouring or second-order tasks.

Study of the material itself comes up with other evidence. Some pieces of equipment, for example, bear a number of different owners' names inscribed or punched on them, showing that serviceable equipment was at least on occasion handed down from soldier to soldier within the regiment. Indeed, no good purpose could have been served by allowing a veteran on retirement to retain his arms and armour. The armoury probably held a store of weapons and uniforms which would be continually refurbished and kept in good repair for re-issue to new recruits.

What, then, is the nature of the material found on a site by the archaeologist of today? Much of the Roman metalwork available for study comes from major hoards found deliberately buried in pits: ironwork and nails at Inchtuthil, armour and horse-trappings from Newstead, parade-armour and cavalry fittings, and a hoard of iron weapons and tools, including swords, daggers, and spearheads, from Künzing. It has been commonly assumed that this material was buried in order to prevent its falling into the hands of an enemy. It is at least as likely, however, that such hoards represented not the unit's stock of serviceable equipment, but a pile of scrap awaiting refurbishment at the hands of the resident craftsmen.

If this hypothesis is correct, views about the production of Roman military equipment may need considerable modification: items found on site will only be chance losses; otherwise the equipment will normally have been deliberately discarded because of irretrievable damage, and would therefore end up on the armourer's heap for melting down. The requirement for new production of military equipment would be consequently diminished, and supplies could be maintained by a few specialist craftsmen supplemented by 'fatigues parties' of men to work the bellows, gather fuel, and do all the fetching and carrying. On the actual assembly line, tasks could be assigned in the same way, the skilled men producing scabbard or belt plates, while the unskilled cut and sewed the leather on which they were fitted.

Armed with accurate information about the material under study, as well as all these other considerations, hypotheses about its production and distribution can be formed – the process of so-called 'model-building', where theoretical situations are matched against evidence from the surviving Roman military equipment to see how far they resemble the picture which has been recorded. By such means, the distance travelled by the material from its production centre, the number of repairs it has undergone, or the length of time it has continued in service before being decommissioned ought to show how valuable or scarce certain items of equipment were. Distribution patterns will begin to define whether equipment used by legionary and auxiliary troops was different, whether it came from separate workshops, and whether the former was more ornate and costly than the latter. Research would begin to narrow down the search for the production centres themselves, or show whether they existed at all, as well as help to define what a military *fabrica* might look like if an archaeologist stumbled across one. Further definition of whereabouts on Roman fort sites the main concentrations of such material had been found would lead to a better understanding of how military equipment found on archaeological sites today should be interpreted.

By a process, therefore, of examining the material, of looking at it as far as possible within its historical context, and on this basis forming an unashamedly up-to-date view of how it may have been produced, marketed, repaired, or abandoned, more historical flesh can be placed on the archaeological bare bones. Interpretations of the material are produced which can be measured against excavated sites and their finds, and used to form research designs for fresh discoveries. They provide insights in various ways into how the ancient economies worked, how production was organized, and, ultimately, how archaeologists of today should better understand the material they handle.

8

The Roman environment

One of the areas where the greatest recent advances have been seen in the gathering of archaeological information is that of environmental studies. Since the earliest days, the ability of men to adapt their lifestyles to take best advantage of natural resources, or to overcome difficulties by a gradual process of changing their surroundings and harnessing the forces of nature, has been a hallmark of progress and a measure of the degree of civilization of their age. In the Roman period as in any other, climate, disease, farming practices, and natural disasters have their effect on the style and quality of life in both town and countryside. Evidence which reflects these aspects of life in the Roman world can be recovered and interpreted by careful excavation and analytical techniques.

There is a sense in which such material is quite different in character from Roman finds and artifacts. Evidence for the Roman environment is part of an unconscious record locked in the soils and deposits which form the matrix for other site-finds. It tends to survive to the present day against all the odds. On the other hand, unless the archaeologist seizes the chance of understanding the broader context of a site, assessing the relationship between it and its surrounding countryside, or using environmental evidence to create a picture of the climate or the quality of life, a complete dimension to an understanding of the past may be missed.

To the casual observer, environmental material often looks unpromising. At its most obvious it comprises bones, both animal and human, which survive well in many types of soil, and other animal by-products, such as leather, ivory, horn, or parchment, which dwell on the border-line between environmental and artifactual material. Plant remains can also survive, usually in conditions where the destructive combination of air and water has been excluded. Thus waterlogged deposits – the bases of Roman ditches or pits on clay sites – can produce a spectacular amount of wood, plant, and other organic remains, and arid, airless sites, such as sealed caves or tombs in the desert lands of Egypt or the Near East, can on occasion contain parchments and papyri, or objects such as wooden coffins and their mummified contents.

The correct conditions can act as preservative for a host of other types of evidence, many of which are far more resilient than one might expect. Seeds, for example, and traces of pollens and plant remains can be preserved, sometimes carbonized within burnt deposits, sometimes in waterlogged conditions or in certain types of peaty soils. By a painstaking process these can be sifted from their surrounding earth and examined. The remains of some insects – the hard wing-cases of beetles, and microscopic portions of other insects – can on occasion be studied in the same way. More durable and common site-finds are the shells of snails and gastropods of all kinds. Finally, the soil itself, in which all this material is found, has always been deposited on its site by some means or other. It is normally itself of organic origin, and it too will probably contain traces of spores, pollens, and possibly seeds which are contemporary with the formation of the deposit and which may give clues as to the prevailing conditions at the time of deposition.

This may give the impression that the archaeologist cannot afford to ignore any of the site he is excavating, and in one sense this is true. But it is also impractical and expensive to give the highest degree of attention to every crumb of soil. Work on seeds, soils, and pollens is normally focused on areas where there are seen to be deposits with a high degree of survival, or as part of a sampling strategy carried out throughout the site. Analysis of promising layers and deposits normally takes place by extracting a block of soil and immersing it in a flotation chamber, thus releasing seeds and other environmental material which float to the top. These deposits can then be examined under whatever magnification is required to identify species by comparison with modern-day examples.

Fundamental to an understanding of the environment of the site is the nature of the soil, and, ironically, this is precisely the portion of the site which many archaeologists tend somewhat unthinkingly to throw away. The archaeologist needs to be as well informed as possible about how deposits of soil on the site have been built up. It will be of significance, for example, to know if ditches have been deliberately filled or whether they have gradually silted: environmental evidence may be used to suggest how long they remained open. An early example of the kind of argument deployed on the basis of environmental remains is found in the report on excavations in 1928 at the fort of Birdoswald on Hadrian's Wall. Here, samples of seeds from the lower portions of the waterlogged ditch of the vallum were analysed by an expert botanist. They were found to consist only of knot-grass, chickweed, and buttercup, which, as any gardener knows, are the weeds which most quickly colonize new areas of waste or disturbed ground. In this case, the identification of these seeds backed up the excavators' impression, gained from the nature of the filling of the ditch, that it had been quickly and deliberately backfilled soon after it was first opened.

More comprehensive use of environmental material from a variety of

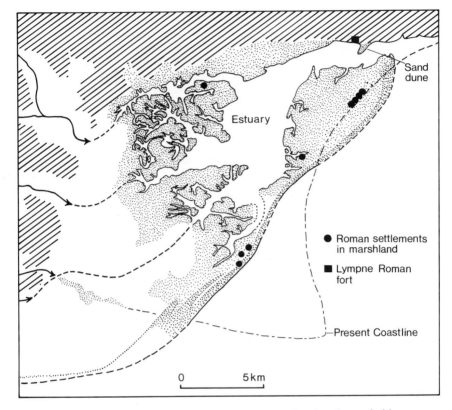

Figure 35 Map of Lympne and its surrounding area, showing the probable coastline in the Roman period

soils carefully sampled over a wide area was incorporated in an excavation and survey project at the site of Lympne on the southern coast of Britain. Here, the tumbled remains of a substantial walled enclosure of late Roman date still stand at the foot of a hill, virtually at the level of marshlands which lie between it and the sea. The site is known as one of the forts of the Roman coastal defensive system which formed the 'Saxon Shore', and material connected with the British naval force, the Classis Britannica of earlier Roman days, has also been found there. In addressing the task of discovering the relationship that this site, now two miles inland, had with the sea in the Roman period, archaeologists had recourse to two forms of information about the deposits of soils in the area, one geological and the other environmental.

A map showing the results of a soil survey of the area indicated that the marsh deposits were of two kinds. Part was apparently a shingle spit which formed the seaward edge of the marsh, and which may have already started forming in the Roman period. The rest, the inner portion, was a silty estuarine deposit, on the edge of which stood the Roman fort site. Its position for this seemed to have been particularly well chosen: it was protected behind a tongue of land forming a sand-bar between it and what must have been the seaward mouth of the estuary. This led to the suggestion that the site lay at the mouth of a river which has since substantially changed its course, but which in the Roman period reached the English Channel via a major open estuary, protected from the open sea by the shingle spit. At the mouth of the river stood the Roman installation, ideally placed to patrol the seas, provide a safe harbour, and control access to the inner reaches of the southern part of Britain.

Corroboration of these findings came from environmental samples taken from the supposed Roman shore-lines at the foot of the slope on which the Roman site lies. Above layers of shingle buried deep in the modern marsh, a thick layer of black organic clay was found, and, above this, layers of estuarine silts. Samples of diatoms, microscopic water-living algae, from both the beach and the organic clay, were those of organisms which favour a saline environment. This clearly showed that at the time when they were deposited the area was an open marine estuary protected by its shingle beach. This discovery helped strengthen the excavators' understanding of the positioning and context of the site which they were studying. In this case, a conjunction of environmental and geological information has enabled a new interpretation of the way in which a large tract of marshland in southern Britain has been formed to be put forward with some confidence.

In striving to understand their site and its context – particularly if, like a Roman villa or farm, it is one which must have relied to a very great extent on the productivity of the land around it – excavators can hardly ignore what the soils in the area can tell them. This can help reveal the density of settlement which the land supported, or the extent and the quality in the Roman period of land which farms and villas were seeking to exploit. Evidence which has a bearing on these questions can come from geological surveys of the soils as they are at present, though it must always be borne in mind that the quality of land and its productiveness can alter dramatically depending on the uses to which it is put; good soils of today were not necessarily so in the Roman period. Further information can also come from the recognition and analysis of pollens deposited at a date contemporary with the use of the sites themselves or from other environmental evidence of all kinds – animal bones, insect or mollusc remains. From these a picture of the composition of the surrounding flora and fauna is built up, which in turn helps to give an indication of the sorts of species and preferred habitats which were available in the area in the Roman period. This, too, begins to define the climate and character of the surroundings at the time.

Much of the gathering of evidence for conclusions of this nature is painstakingly slow. In seeking to understand why a concentration of farm-steads and settlements of Roman date, recorded by aerial photography or field-walking in the highland zones of Britain, lie in the area in which they do, one theory may suggest that this land must have been relatively productive at the time, and that the group of settlements is evidence of large-scale commercial exploitation, perhaps aimed at supplying *annona* to Roman troops on frontier duty. Conversely, it could also be argued that the remains are no more than evidence of a subsistence economy. Each small farmstead may not have held a vast acreage of land, and in a relatively hostile environment – a coastal marshland or upland zone – a number of small discrete settlements, each with a restricted holding of land which barely provided the occupant with enough capacity for subsistence-level production, could be mistaken for evidence of wide-scale exploitation. An archaeological method of determining which of these theories is the more likely to be correct would be to carry out a programme of investigation, which would have to include the analysis of soil types in an attempt to determine how they had formed, excavation of settlement sites, and environmental sampling both of the sites themselves and their surroundings in an attempt to build up something of a picture of the climate, the landscape, and the extent of man's influence on his immediate surroundings. Without an amalgamation of excavation, artifactual, and environmental evidence, informed interpretation of the patterns of Roman settlement is next to impossible.

One of the commonest site-finds, second perhaps only to pottery, is animal bone. Properly handled and interpreted, this provides the raw data whereby the excavator can understand the character of the site or the habits and agricultural practices of its occupants. In contrast to other environmental material, bones are often large enough to be noticed and thus easily collected during the course of excavation. This is not always the case, for although the bones of larger animals, like cattle, sheep, or pigs, are of a size which is not easy to miss, the bones of slighter mammals or birds and fish are of a different order altogether, and could easily not be seen on excavation, or may not survive so well. A full sampling and recovery strategy will result in identification and evaluation of the full range of bones which have been deposited on the site.

Animal bones can generally be taken as indicators of one of a number of different aspects of man's use of animals, depending on the types of site where they are found. If the bones come from the site of a Roman farm or villa, their study will help to determine as far as is possible the stock levels of the Roman farm, the relative proportions and sexes of different species represented, and the age at which animals were generally culled for food production. From the study of tooth wear and the analysis of certain bones which only fuse into their fully adult shape at known stages of an animal's progress towards maturity, it may be possible to chart the age at death of certain species, male and female. Examining sheep bones in this way may help to determine whether wool production was an important factor in the economy of the farm, or whether it was primarily a food-producing unit. In order to make judgements of this kind, it is always necessary to have a good and well-stratified series of samples of material available for study, preferably of contemporary or near contemporary date, for farming practices, like anything else, can change with the times. It is thus important for the consultant who is to identify the animal bones to be kept well up-to-date with the excavator's overall concept of the development of the site, so that the study of the bones is an integral factor and an informed contribution to the understanding of the site's development and use.

On an urban site, or on one associated with the Roman military, animal bones would not normally be regarded as having any direct bearing on farming practice; in urban rubbish contexts, they would be seen as evidence for diet. Here, study of the bones would perhaps concentrate on other aspects, in viewing the sorts of joints found in terms of their economic value, as indicators of the dietary preferences of the inhabitants, and as the consumer end of a cycle of production. Bones can be studied for signs of how the carcasses were cut up, to determine whether whole carcasses arrived at the site for distribution, or whether the meat came ready jointed into preferred cuts. At the other end of the scale, some indication can also be gained of the methods for disposal of rubbish, perhaps by seeing whether the bones had been gnawed by dogs, or by finding bones of pests (e.g. rats) mixed in with other deposits. In this way, a picture of the bustling markets in a town, or the rations doled out to hungry soldiers in a frontier post, can be built up, and indications received about the production and supply mechanisms which supported this structure.

The use of animal products was sometimes part of an industrial concern. Workshops using bone, horn, or ivory required a ready supply of suitable material, and the sources for this, how the rest of the carcass was disposed of, as well as the portions of the various animals which were necessary for this sort of production will be of interest. More generally, analysis of the bone finds from a series of well-stratified Roman sites should give clear indications of the sorts of species and sizes of stock commonly found at various places within the Roman provinces. This will contribute to a picture of Roman farming practices which can be matched against accounts of Roman writers on the subject of farming such as Pliny and Columella.

Bone finds on sites often include a proportion of bones of non-domestic animals, or of animals which may also have been kept as pets or for other purposes. Bird bones identified at the Roman fort site of Valkenburg in Holland included not only various forms of edible fowl, but species as diverse as the crow, petrel, cormorant, heron, crane, and white-tailed eagle. Elsewhere, the bones of small mammals reveal the spread of pests, and give further indication of the standards of cleanliness which were the norm at a particular site. Lastly, the bones of wild animals – boar, bear, or deer – found at a site allow a glimpse to be had of the sorts of countryside or habitat around the site in question, and possibly also of the forms of leisure pursuits favoured by the inhabitants.

Human remains are of a different order. Burial in an orderly fashion was the standard practice of the Romans, and where this does not seem to have occurred, the event is of some significance, and may give rise to lurid theories. In one of the buildings outside the Roman fort of Housesteads on Hadrian's Wall, for example, excavators discovered the bones of an adult male buried under a laid clay floor. Since this burial appeared to have taken place in secret, without making use of the main cemetery area of the fort, the excavators immediately, and with some justification, gave the house the name 'Murder House'.

The excavation of a cemetery can give a great deal of information about the people of the Roman provinces – their physical appearance, their prosperity, sometimes even their superstitions, fears, or beliefs. Within the physical remains of human corpses it is possible to identify the traces of disease, to estimate tooth wear (as an indication of diet), to study any surgery or dentistry they may have undergone, and to assess any deformities caused by occupational hazards and their general state of nutrition at death. It is also on occasion possible to distinguish distinct racial or generic types, perhaps from shape of heads or from the overall size of bodies. In the late Roman cemetery at Lankhills, Winchester, for example, the excavator was able to distinguish a group of burial remains in the very latest phases which were physically very different from all the other occupants of the cemetery: this he explained historically by suggesting that these men were the mercenary soldiers drafted into Winchester from the Germanic nations to help garrison the city at a time when law and order within the province of Britain was on the brink of breaking down.

Pathological studies of the bones from cemetery excavations can be exceptionally revealing. In one of the cemeteries at Cirencester, lying near the amphitheatre of the Roman city, examination of the bones revealed that of 239 individuals whose age could be roughly determined, the average age at death for males was 40.8 years, while for females it was 37.8. Tooth decay was not a very prevalent factor, probably due to a diet which was rich in meat but low in starches and sugars; by modern standards, however, the amount of wear was heavy. By far the majority of individuals in the cemetery showed signs, sometimes severe, of osteoarthritis – strain on the bones and joints of the body from the normal wear and tear of heavy manual labour. This all contributes to a view of the quality of life in a normal Roman city during the course of the second century. The number of individuals who appeared to have suffered severe wounds, some of which may have been the cause of death, was surprising. The interpretation of this sort of evidence is always a leap into the dark: could it have been that life was violent then, or does the excavated cemetery contain the bodies of those unfortunates who met their end in the amphitheatre nearby?

Questions like these cannot be answered with any certainty, but the contribution of environmental evidence to the picture of the life of individuals in the Roman world is worth stressing. The examination of the cemetery of a Roman fort will reveal much of great significance for the understanding of the Roman army and its relationship to civilians. Study of burials, whether they are cremations or inhumations, will show the extent to which family life formed a normal part of the soldier's way of living, the proportion of men who died in service, or the number of men who stayed on in the area of their former fort when they reached the age of retirement as veterans. When this can be linked, as at Lankhills in Winchester, with a particular form of uniform or equipment, information of this nature will give direct evidence about the composition and organization of the Roman army, the living conditions of the soldiers on campaign and at their leisure, their life-expectancy, the rigours (and perhaps also the consolations) of frontier duties.

A number of particular environmental circumstances provide ideal conditions for the survival of organic remains. In areas which have been waterlogged since the Roman period, remains of plants and wood are commonly recovered. A particularly rich assortment of such material recovered from waterlogged deposits at the Roman fort of Vindolanda near Hadrian's Wall, and dating from the late first or early second century AD, shows the extent to which our understanding of material from other sites is of necessity less than complete. Not only did these deposits contain shovels, axles, tent-pegs, bowls, and plates, among dozens of other interesting artifacts – all material which normally is never found because it is perishable – but also a mass of writing-tablets, forming part of an archive apparently kept in the office of the commander of the camp. Decipherment of these handwritten messages, some of them dealing with the supply of foodstuffs or other requisitions for the fort, others more personal documents, has proved an invaluable source of information on the Roman ordnance and administrative systems and has highlighted some of the social factors at work in the Roman army on garrison duty. As artifacts, too, these wooden finds, carved out of living materials, give sound evidence for the Roman environment at the time of the fort's occupation, as well as information about the standards of craftsmanship in wood to which the Roman army was used.

Evidence from leaves, twigs, seeds, and pollens can build up into a

Figure 36 (a) Leather horse chamfron, with some bronze decorations surviving; (b) Child's sock, sewn together from a textile offcut. Both finds come from waterlogged deposits at Vindolanda, dated *c.*AD100

broad picture of the climate, the vegetation, and the environment in the Roman period. The presence of grape or fig pips on a site, however, cannot necessarily be taken to mean that the climate was mild enough to support tender fruits of this kind: one needs to find examples of roots or branches from the vine or the fig to be certain that husbandry of these plants was carried out at the site under examination. Waterlogged layers

135

will often retain seeds and pollens of many forms of plant found in the neighbourhood of the site; by studying the proportions of these represented in selected samples of environmental deposits, it will often be possible to suggest whether the surrounding land was wooded or arable, whether there was water nearby, and whether the prevailing temperatures were warmer or cooler than those of today.

It is often useful to attempt to build these sorts of detailed observations into a more general picture of Roman practice in a particular area of husbandry. The Roman timber supply, vital as a fuel for baths, industry, pottery manufacture, and production of metals and glass, must have been highly efficient and well organized. In Britain at least, there is at present no evidence that the proportion of woodland to arable or open land in the Roman period was substantially different from that of today, and finds of pollens from Roman sites suggest that the general aspect of the countryside was in many respects very similar, though one must assume that there were large areas of afforested land in areas not covered today which have since dwindled considerably due to the encroachment of modern agricultural practice and the demands of industry. Timber, both for fuel and for building, was clearly in great demand, and the collection of environmental evidence from sites is one of the more productive avenues of research which may eventually lead to more information on how its husbandry was planned and organized. Roman historical sources suggest that professional forestry and woodcraft were well known in Italy; they were probably also practised in Britain, but it is only from the collection of wood samples from Roman sites, the identification of artifacts and timbers to determine the sorts of woods used in various ways, and the analysis of charcoals in burnt deposits, together with the identification of pollens, which will build up a corpus of information about the supply and use of timber.

In constructing a complete picture of a site, it is normally necessary also to use evidence from insect and mollusc remains. Insect wing-cases are formed of hard, skeletal material which is difficult to destroy, and snail-shells are virtually indestructible. Each form of insect or mollusc alive in the Roman period has remained in a virtually unaltered form to the present day, and the modern species prefer foods and habitats which one may assume to have been similar in the Roman period. Thus the microscopic remains of insects and molluscs can provide a very clear indicator of the microclimate, the ambient conditions, and the habitats in the sites where they are found. Among the best indicators are different species of beetles. Study of seventy-six different species found in a deposit within the Roman fort at Neuss, in Germany, suggested that, according to their known preferences for habitat, the area in which they were discovered must have been fairly damp, with plenty of rotting vegetation and animal dung, and a high proportion of fresh weeds and grasses. This accorded well with the theory that the nearby buildings must have been stables, where all these conditions would apply.

In complete contrast, the remains of beetles discovered in Roman buildings, probably riverside warehouses, belonging to the late first and early second centuries AD at York allowed a different interpretation of the environmental evidence. Two phases of timber structures were identified on the site, separated by a layer of humic silt, which contained a wide variety of insect remains. Over this was dumped a further layer of cleaner clay. Biological examination of the remains of the humic layer showed that almost all of the many millions of beetle remains were those of known cereal pests; although cereal remains themselves were not found in any great quantities, there seems little doubt that this site was a grain-store which had become totally contaminated by insects. The only way for the Roman authorities to prevent the contamination from spreading any further was to demolish the store, cover the infected layer with a layer of clean clay and begin building again. This kind of problem may have been more common in the Roman world than we might imagine, and could explain, for example, the charred remains of grain associated with insect remains at other military sites. Care has to be exercised in the interpretation of this sort of evidence: it has often in the past seemed all too easy to assume that a burnt layer or building within a Roman fort was the result of enemy action, and to link its presence with known – that is historically attested – military action. If contamination of cereal warehouses was commonly solved by the Roman army by burning them down and beginning again, what has in the past been construed as 'evidence' for military calamity clearly has to be examined a great deal more closely. Historical accounts of invasions and calamities constructed on the basis of this sort of destruction deposit at particular sites, or at closely identifiable dates, may not be all they seem.

Environmental samples can be used to provide the material for a number of scientific dating techniques. These are rarely as accurate for the Roman period as the pinpoint dating of a pottery vessel by its name-stamp or its style of decoration to the period of production of a known craftsman or workshop. They are on occasion well worthwhile, particularly where they provide a relative date for a class of material – human bones in a cemetery – which, without association with other objects, are impossible to date. Available dating methods separate into those derived from measuring the natural radioactive decay which occurs in all organic material from the time of its deposition in the ground, and those which measure and compare the patterns of the annual growth cycle of timbers found on archaeological sites in an attempt to determine the date at which they were cut down.

Radiocarbon dating is based on detailed work on one of the rarer radioactive isotopes of carbon, so-called carbon-14, which occurs naturally at a constant level in the atmosphere. It is absorbed by all living creatures during the course of their lifetime, keeping this constant level of radioactive carbon topped up. On burial in the ground, and after removal from exposure to natural atmospheric radiation, radiocarbon isotopes begin to decay at a steady rate, losing their radioactivity in the process. For convenience's sake, the rate of decay of this isotope is measured against a 'half life', the length of time it takes to lose half of its radioactivity, measured, in the case of carbon-14, as 5,730 plus or minus 40 years. Since levels of natural radiation have remained constant for many thousands of years, measurements of the amount of radiation stored in a piece of bone from an animal or wood from a tree of today can be compared with a similar sample from an archaeological deposit. The age of the archaeological sample can be determined by very accurate recording of the amount of radiation loss it has undergone and by thus determining how close the sample is to the point, at about 5,730 years old, when it will have lost half of its radioactivity.

The method relies for its accuracy on the selection for study of samples which have been protected since their deposition within the ground from the contaminant effects of further radiation from the atmosphere. Even so, very sophisticated machinery is required to measure accurately the small amounts of this rare carbon-14 isotope. The process can only produce a date which is accurate in terms of probabilities rather than certainties, and there is always a margin of possible error. Results from a fragment of wood from a deposit of the Roman period submitted for testing might therefore be presented in a form something like this: 'The sample submitted has a 60 per cent chance of being 1,750 plus or minus 40 years old, and a 90 per cent chance of being 1,750 plus or minus 80 years old.' Thus although the mean point of our sample lies 1,750 years ago, at AD200 (all radiocarbon dates are calculated before present, which is standardized at 1950), the outside limits of the possible date-range can only be fixed between AD120 and 280, and even then there is still a one in ten chance that this is incorrect. Since a range as expanded as this spans a great deal of the historical period of the Roman Empire, these sorts of conclusions may not be a great deal of use in themselves to archaeologists of the Roman period who may be able to rely on more accurate dating for their material by other means.

Tree-ring dating, on the other hand, affords the prospect of much greater accuracy. The process works by the collection of timber samples, measuring their annual growth rings with microscopic exactitude, and matching the statistical pattern obtained to a general pattern for tree growth in the area within the relevant historical period. The size of the annual ring of timber which each tree forms is a product of climatic conditions, which can be assumed to have been reasonably consistent within each local area. By careful matching, a series of measurements of the normal annual growth-rate of trees in particular areas can be established, and, once pegged by a number of securely dated examples, can be built on by new samples from trees or timber that partially overlap and augment the known and established sequences. This in turn enables samples from undated sites to be fitted as consistently as possible within the series of established measurements, thus making it possible to assign them a date by reference to the others.

There are drawbacks to this form of dating. The most serious is that the process relies to a certain extent upon a circular argument: it is not possible to tie the annual rate of growth of the control sample of trees to a specific year without being certain from securely dated archaeological contexts that the tested samples themselves are accurately dated by historically derived means. Precise dating of this nature is ultimately reached by a combination of archaeological and historical evidence – itself often a tenuous link, but one which becomes more secure the more it is supported by further independent evidence which points to the same conclusion. In the case of tree-ring dating, which offers a relatively exact method of arranging a series of wood samples into a reliable sequence, it is perfectly possible to build up a pattern of annual tree-growth into which all the samples fit without being able to tie this to an exact date derived through some historical link.

Two further drawbacks remain. First, the dating method relies for its validity on consistent climatic conditions producing a similar reaction among trees within their region. Apparently small differences in the rainfall pattern can affect the microclimate even within related areas, and can throw up anomalous timbers which might distort the emerging patterns – or themselves be wrongly dated. Second, as with any artifact, it is always necessary to look at the archaeological context within which it is found. Timber used in the construction of a building may have been cut down specially for use where it is found: in this case, once due allowance has been made for a period of seasoning, the felling date will be close to the construction date of the building. All too often, however, it may be the case that timber, a valuable commodity in its own right, was put to secondary use and can always therefore be considerably older than the date of the structure or the archaeological context in which it is found.

Like many other forms of archaeological examination, the study of the past environment involves painstaking, detailed, and very specialist work. It must rely on the accurate identification of seeds or pollens under a microscope or precise measurement of tree-rings or of the sizes of animal bones, followed by a number of statistical analyses of the results. These are rarely spectacular enough to hit the archaeological headlines, but the gradual incorporation of the results of this work into emerging archaeological understanding can lead to new methods of looking at old material or the overturning of old misconceptions.

Recent research, relying heavily on environmental material, on the gardens of the Roman town of Pompeii has produced new evidence of a sort which had never been thought possible before. Re-excavation, coupled with the recognition and identification of planting systems and seeds within the old Roman ground surface, has made it possible to reconstruct some of the garden plans in unexpected detail. The technique relies on the peculiar conditions prevailing at the time that Pompeii was buried: gardens as well as houses were covered by the rain of small stones from Vesuvius; this meant that trees and shrubs eventually decayed in the soil where they had grown, and the tree-roots formed cavities. Raised garden beds, or other relatively slight formations of the garden soil, can often be recovered by means of careful excavation down to the original ground surface, as can the sites of planting in pots or the positions of fountains or other special arrangements. Once the garden level has been established, tree-cavities within the ground surface can be easily recognized, and by pouring plaster into them, a visual identification of the sort of tree planted at each spot can be attempted. In addition, a careful search of the old ground surface itself has often revealed carbonized seeds or fruit pips, further evidence of the types of trees and other vegetation in the gardens.

Typical of Pompeii is the peristyle garden in the House of Julius Polybius. Examination revealed that there were five main trees within a small area, two of which had roots similar to those of figs, two others seemed to be fruit trees, perhaps cherry or pear, while the last was apparently an olive. Along one of the garden walls was evidence of a series of pots which had contained further small trees – possibly lemons. Across the middle of the garden, and recoverable only as a soil-mark where it had charred away in the heat from the eruption of Vesuvius, was a ladder, about eight metres long, and tapering towards its top. This was dramatic evidence of the number of fruit trees in a garden of this size, and of their size and productivity. Further evidence of the sorts of gardens that town-dwellers felt were desirable, even if these did not actually exist in Pompeii, comes from wall-paintings in the House of the Fruit Orchard. Here, the rich wall-decorations include trees laden with fruit of all sorts – cherries, yellow and purple plums, pears, pomegranates, grapes, strawberries, and lemons. These are interspersed with a wide variety of flowers and birds, including many identifiable species.

Gardens of all sizes were examined as part of the project, and many showed signs of the outdoor life that went on. One of the modest-sized gardens on the Via de Nocera contained a small triclinium, an arrangement of three couches round a central table for outdoor dining, with a serving table nearby. Post-holes in the area showed that there was a pergola to afford shade, and roots next to the posts were identifiable as vines. Examination of the soils around the triclinium produced a number

Figure 37 Plans of gardens at Pompeii: (a) the market garden orchard; (b) the vineyard ('Forum Boarium'); see *Figure 2*, nos 14 and 12 respectively.
Key: A Vegetable beds; B Basins and cisterns; C Dining areas
Dots indicate roots of grapevines, and larger dots or circles the sites of larger trees

of clam shells and animal bones, suggesting that meals al fresco were not necessarily tidy occasions. In the remainder of the garden, there were twenty-five other trees – probably olives, with larger main trees round the edges. There were indications that the spaces between the trees were used for vegetable growing: the minute examination of the garden soil revealed the remains of pulses.

More spectacular was the examination of a large area north of the amphitheatre, which had always been known as the 'Forum Boarium', the cattle market. Excavation within this large area, measuring some 75 by 84 metres, revealed that, far from being an empty space in AD79, this was filled with plants laid out in a pattern typical of what one would expect in a vineyard. Within the area available for study, amounting perhaps to two-thirds of the enclosure, over 1,400 vines were planted in strict rows, at 1.2 m centres, with a central criss-cross path. There were two dining areas within this large area, one of them in close association with what appeared to be an establishment producing and selling wine. Analysis of seeds and other carbonized fruit remains from this vineyard showed that as well as vines there were probably a large number of fruit-trees, the roots of fifty-eight of which were identified on excavation, and which included filberts and walnuts. Reassessment of the animal bones discovered at the site at the time of original excavation has revealed that the 'cattle market' was far more likely to have been an open-air wine-bar and restaurant, in which diners could sit on couches outdoors among vines, olives, and other fruit and nut trees to consume favourite joints of meat.

Work on the gardens at Pompeii, with its variety of techniques including excavation, analysis of seeds and pollens from Roman ground surfaces, and the identification of trees and other plants from their root-casts, has altered our picture of the nature of the town-dweller's outdoor life in this small town in the Campanian countryside in the first century AD. It has shown that within the walls of Pompeii there were vineyards, outdoor wine-bars, market gardens, allotments, and possibly even horticultural establishments supplying cut flowers. It has enabled more evidence for Roman gardening techniques and practices to be built up, and shown the considerable interest which can lie for the archaeologist in seemingly empty spaces within the Roman town.

Detailed environmental data of this type can be recovered from most individual sites, and help to compile a picture of the climatic conditions, the surrounding landscape, potential land-uses, and the local animal and plant husbandry. The examination of overall themes, however, enables comparisons to be drawn between sites throughout the breadth of the Roman Empire. In areas where conquest was followed by the implantation of towns, study of the environmental remains may point to traces of earlier settlement or pre-existing farming practices in the area, or may sketch a picture of the topography, vegetation, and land-uses as well as determine how this altered, if at all, when the Romans arrived. For towns or villas, it will be of interest to study the food supply, the economic base of the settlement, and any evidence from the landscape of the amount of agricultural activity in the local area. Cross-provincial study of these aspects of the Roman world will ultimately prove fruitful in under-standing the economic and social processes at work, and will focus on the areas where, in what was largely a pre-industrial society, wealth – in the form of agricultural productivity – was concentrated.

It is in the definition of what happened in the immediate post-Roman period that environmental archaeology can perhaps make a significant contribution. In a period when the lack of a strong central authority caused political and economic instability, work on the environmental record should be able to show whether settlements came abruptly to an end, whether the economic and farming base changed in any significant way, and what were the quality and form of sub-Roman or post-Roman city-dwellers' lifestyles. If there was a failure of agriculture, significant under-cultivation of land, or a marked population decline in the immediate post-Roman period, pollen analysis should show significant regeneration of woodland areas to be occurring sufficiently, within about fifty years, to overtake abandoned sites of settlements or villas. Examination of aspects such as these, hardly touched on at all by the writers of the time, affords greater prospects of fresh advances in our understanding of what was taking place at this crucial period than further squeezing of historical texts to extract the last drops of distilled narrative history.

Just as evidence from environmental materials cannot stand in isolation from consideration of the distribution of sites and artifacts, and the relative wealth or poverty of the sites under examination, so conclusions drawn from other types of archaeological material ignore evidence about their environmental surroundings at their peril. Our archaeological picture of the Roman past is increasingly a jigsaw of pieces resulting from work which relies upon techniques developed to study different classes of evidence in ways which will maximize the information they can impart. Not only do these show a series of individual facets of Roman society often ignored by the historical sources, but they are increasingly interrelating to produce new, and sometimes dramatically different, views of the forces at work in the Roman past.

9

The potential of archaeology

It will already have become clear that the archaeologist of today is able to make use of a battery of techniques and methods of studying the material remains of the past. These include many processes borrowed from other disciplines which help to sharpen awareness of what limitations the evidence has, and what conclusions can legitimately be drawn from it. While archaeologists concentrating on other periods, primarily prehistoric, have been among the first to apply these forms of study to sites and artifacts which do not readily fit into a well-dated framework, the benefits of these sorts of approach are beginning to be appreciated in the study of the Roman period.

It is not possible to run through the whole range of available techniques, nor to give examples of all the ways in which Roman archaeology might benefit from or is already taking advantage of these methods of study. Certain examples, however, do stand out: one can point to the classification of artifacts by the use of computer techniques, the employment of sampling methods for surveys of widespread geographical areas, and the application of other techniques used to assess the human geography of an area, and which can use the data from the Roman period as readily as today's statistics.

A study of Roman spear-head types which took seven standard measuring points on each example (the length, the greatest breadth, the diameter of the shaft at two points, and so on) has demonstrated the usefulness of computer-based sorting methods in assigning the various spears studied into family groups. Relationships between them were shown diagrammatically, rather like a family tree, in which the main trunk represented the basic starting point (that each object was a spear-head) and began to branch out into various directions depending on the likeness to each other of different groups of spears represented. Thus, wider, rounder spear-heads were assigned to a different family group from long, thin ones. Although using a computer to sort this material was of great help in showing where the main areas of similarity or difference lay, and in giving as objective a classification of them as possible, a great many value judgements still had to be made in deciding which of the recorded differences between spear-heads or spear types were important and which could be disregarded.

Sampling can be a convenient short cut to reaching valid conclusions from a large amount of evidence, whether this is animal bone or pottery from a site with prolific finds, or whether it is a field survey whose aim is to analyse the settlement pattern in a large geographical area. It is important, however, to be certain about what is meant by a sample. It would not be true, for example, to say that most museums contain a valid statistical sample of Roman material from their local sites and areas; a great deal of selectivity has usually gone into the formation of museum collections. What is in their stores may be biased towards the interesting, the impressive, or the easily recognizable, rather than forming a really representative sample of the sorts of material of Roman date available locally. On occasion, it may even be necessary to excavate a site by sampling it, normally immediately prior to its destruction; here a quick excavation may extract information rapidly from a restricted but well-selected area – just sufficient to give some glimpse of what the whole might have been.

Statistical sampling relies on obtaining a random selection of the material under study. This is perhaps best achieved in landscape surveys of regions in an attempt to determine the frequency or the nature of archaeological sites and thus the patterns of past settlement in a given area. Instead of looking in detail at the whole of a large tract of land, smaller areas are selected; these are normally either squares or strips, located either at random or in a regular pattern to cover the zone of interest.

It is often impractical to be totally objective about the choice of survey area and those carrying out the survey often have to accept the best possible compromise. A recent piece of work on sites of the Roman period in the south of France between Toulon and Fréjus is a case in point. This land, the Permian basin, formed a good agricultural zone within one of the earliest areas of Roman influence outside Italy. The upland areas, where Iron Age and later Roman sites appear to have lain, were densely forested, difficult to survey, and pierced only by occasional hunting tracks. The more open hill-slopes were more productive, and produced several settlements and villas of Roman date, though they, too, were more difficult to survey, mainly because of the presence of modern villas, the equivalent of their Roman predecessors. The plain itself was productive, though because much of it is covered by vineyards which are cultivated in traditional ways, there is always the possibility of pottery and other artifacts being dragged some distance out of the context of the site to which they belonged. Despite these difficulties, the survey has shown the potential, discovered many new sites, and given a sample of the sorts of settlement patterns of Roman date to be found in the area.

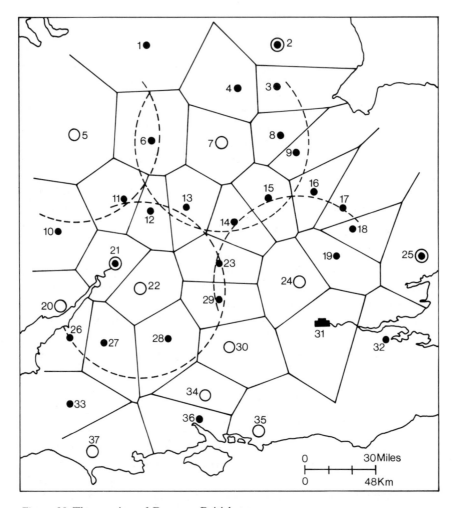

Figure 38 The spacing of Romano-British towns
1 Buxton; 2 Lincoln; 3 Ancaster; 4 Thorpe; 5 Wroxeter; 6 Wall; 7 Leicester;
8 Great Casterton; 9 Water Newton; 10 Kenchester; 11 Droitwich; 12 Alcester;
13 Chesterton; 14 Towcester; 15 Irchester; 16 Godmanchester; 17 Cambridge;
18 Great Chesterford; 19 Braughing; 20 Caerwent; 21 Gloucester; 22 Cirencester;
23 Alchester; 24 St Albans; 25 Colchester; 26 Sea Mills; 27 Bath; 28 Mildenhall;
29 Dorchester; 30 Silchester; 31 London; 32 Rochester; 33 Ilchester;
34 Winchester; 35 Chichester; 36 Bitterne; 37 Dorchester

Study techniques developed by geographers can also be used to determine the character of the settlement pattern within an area. The so-called central place theory is based on the definition of central towns or villages which offer a range of services to their surrounding region. In rural areas, the central places will normally act as markets; they do not compete with each other, but offer a rural community easy access. If all such centres are of equal importance, they will tend to be spaced at equal distances, and each town will serve a circular area around it. Analysis of the pattern of settlement might show whether this 'agricultural market' model is the correct interpretation for the settlement spacing, or whether some other determining factor, e.g. the need to impose a strong administrative structure, is at work.

Study of the spacing and distribution of Romano-British towns in southern England has shown that there is a hierarchy of organization between the *coloniae*, the cantonal capitals, and the lesser walled towns. The cantonal capitals are regularly spaced, and have intersecting spheres of influence round them with a radius of about fifty kilometres. The lesser towns are clustered on the borders of these areas between the cantonal capitals, normally about thirty kilometres apart. These observations allow various interpretations to be suggested to explain the relative distribution and the relationship between these settlements and towns. The lesser towns may have been sited on the fringes between the larger centres because there they encounterd least competition and satisfied the need of the surrounding population for additional services.

The interest in formulating such theories as these is in comparing known data – the distribution of the towns – with what one might expect if certain theoretical forces were at work. It is often revealing to build theoretical systems or 'models' based on social or economic forces and trends and to compare them with evidence from the past. Conversely, the usefulness of these techniques may be in seeing which of the known settlements do not fit into the pattern suggested by the geographical models, or in using the data for identifying areas where there are unexpected gaps, causing the model to break down. In practical terms this may highlight those areas where further settlements, not yet located, might be expected to lie, and thus can most usefully be sought.

Other examples of a similar sort of model-building have already been encountered in the sections of this book dealing with artifacts and pottery. In examining the distribution patterns of pottery as site-finds from a variety of different places, the archaeologist may compare actual evidence with a series of hypothetical 'models' of how pottery ought to have been distributed given different sets of economic or practical conditions.

Techniques such as these are potentially most valuable when they form part of an attempt to use ancient evidence to reconstruct the Roman patterns of trade, or the comparative wealth or the standards of living of the population. Despite the fact that few such subjects can necessarily be illuminated very well by this method, it is one of the ways in which the archaeologist can approach the problems of understanding how the ancient world worked from evidence which is independent of the written record left by Roman historians or contemporary writers. Past methods of study have tended to concentrate on the archaeological record as a kind of visual aid – a handy means of illuminating what Roman writers said – rather than viewing it from a different direction and finding the means to allow the material to tell its own story.

Evidence for death and burial in the Roman world relies heavily on literary and epigraphic sources: ancient writers describe the rites of burial or the attitude of the mourners, while the epigraphic records on the tombstones themselves speak of the achievements of the deceased while still alive. Archaeological study, however, can supplement this in a number of different ways. It can in a very practical way supplement our picture of Roman attitudes to death revealed by Roman writers. New light can be thrown on ancient beliefs in the classical mythology of the afterlife, on elaborate descriptions of the funeral rites themselves, and on surviving detailed regulations preserved within the law-codes for where and how funerals or burials must be carried out.

Archaeological data come first and foremost from the palaeopathological study of the remains of the individuals themselves. These can not only reveal the age and sex of the deceased, but also diagnose the diseases to which they were most prone, and suggest what was their cause of death. In the case of a woman, it is also often possible to estimate how many children she had borne during her lifetime. If the body has been cremated, such details are harder to come by, but certain key bones may allow identification of male rather than female, and it may still be possible to determine roughly the age of the individual at death.

Second, the evidence in the ground for the ritual or method of burial will be of significance. For an inhumation, the archaeologist will wish to see if there are any traces of a coffin or other receptacle for the corpse, perhaps shown only by the discovery of the iron nails which lay at the corners of the wooden box, or, in more elaborate cases, from the coffin furniture, hinges, handles, or other decoration which is more likely to survive than the wooden box itself. The way the body was laid out for burial, its attitude or position within the grave, the jewellery or other personal ornaments buried at the same time, or even the traces of fabric attached by incrustation to brooches or other metalwork placed within the grave may give sufficient clues to allow a reconstruction of the preparations for disposal of the body or of the burial-rite itself.

Personal objects, pottery, figurines, jugs, or other so-called 'ritual objects' are often found buried with the corpse. Roman burials found in

Britian alone, for example, have been recorded as accompanied by perfume phials, charcoal, egg-shells, lamps, or animal bones, as well as pottery vessels or coins. All these have their possible symbolism which needs to be seen and understood as part of a funerary rite. The egg is a potent symbol of life and rebirth; coins in the deceased's mouth are to pay the ferryman Charon for the last journey across the River Styx to the underworld; charcoal and lamps in the grave may be to light the dead on their journey. Some graves contained the remains of the last meal, perhaps joints of meat provided by the mourners to sustain the deceased on the long last journey into the underworld, and graves are recorded where provision was made through a narrow pipe or funnel for further sustenance or libations to be poured into the grave to help the traveller on his or her way.

Cremations afford less potential for understanding the ritual of burial, though there is some scope for interpretation. Although there are often twisted or charred remains of jewellery or other personal ornaments among the ashes, it is more frequently the burial-urn itself which is of interest. The type of pot in which the survivors chose to lay the last remains of their loved ones may be revealing. A distinction can be drawn between those laid to rest in a brand-new, highly decorated vase, and those who had to be content with something old, worn-out, and simple in style, though what this may mean in social terms is much harder to divine. The type or the form of the vessel, too, may be unusual or out of place within the context of its local area; in this case, it could be suggested either that this was a favourite pot belonging to the deceased, or an heirloom from the attic which was expendable.

Then there must be some consideration given to the way in which the grave was marked on the surface. The poorest of Romans might be buried with no visible sign at all of their resting place. Mass burials, perhaps occasioned by plague or epidemic, were discovered in Rome during the course of the nineteenth century. Thousands of human corpses had been thrown into the ditch fronting Servius Tullius's wall, apparently with little or no ceremony. This may have been the fate always awaiting the urban poor, mass disease or not.

Other excavated cemeteries show the expectations of other classes of society. At Ostia, for example, three main areas of tombs have been studied in some detail. The normal pattern appears to be that a burial-plot outside the town, probably lining one of the main roads, was purchased by inhabitants of the towns during their lifetime. In early imperial days at least, this was the place where the funerary rite itself took place, and where the tomb monument was constructed. Certain common forms of tomb, apparently popular at different times, have been distinguished at Ostia. In the Augustan period, they are either a plain rectangular enclosure, marked perhaps by screens of stone, which sometimes contained a monument to the dead man or woman. By the end of the Augustan period, a new fashion had begun, and the ashes of the dead (cremation was still the norm) were placed in a building known as a *columbarium*, which contained niches to house all the members of a family who would eventually lie in it. Over the years, these gradually became more and more richly decorated. The boundaries of these burial-plots were all well marked, and it is clear from surviving inscriptions from Ostia and elsewhere that the violation of or encroachment on a tomb was considered a very serious matter indeed. Strangely, at Ostia, despite the examination of considerable areas of the cemeteries which lay close to the town, there are few traces of lavish tombs belonging to men from the topmost rank of society. These appear to have lain even further from the centre of the town; in this case, distance from the living was felt to be some kind of indicator of social status.

The form and decoration of the tomb can be taken as an indicator of the status, wealth, beliefs, or tastes of the deceased or of the deceased's family. At one extreme are the monumental tombs of the emperors, which include Augustus's Mausoleum, built in 28BC for himself and his family; Trajan's Column, not intended perhaps as a funerary monument, but which received the ashes of the emperor at his death; and the Mausoleum of Hadrian, so large that it was converted in medieval times into the Castello San Angelo, and even in the late Roman period was considered as a fortified bridgehead for Hadrian's bridge across the Tiber. Further down the scale are monuments such as those left by Gaius Cestius, a contemporary of Augustus, whose pyramid tomb still stands outside the Porta Ostiensis at Rome. Many men and women of substance left a lasting memorial either in the form of a classical monument or in a structure or tombstone which commemorated their former occupation. It was common to find the funerary monument reflecting the life of the deceased; the tomb of a baker, M Vergileius Eurysacis, dating to the first century BC, erected outside the Porta Maggiore at Rome, stands on a series of vertical cylinders (suggested to be corn-measures) and the upper portion bears a number of gaping round holes, perhaps representing the open doors of a bank of bakers' ovens. This is only one of the more massive examples of the many memorials and tombstones which show the deceased engaged in an everyday trade or occupation. Some were clearly very costly and elaborate: the column at Igel, which commemorates the members of a single cloth-making and trading family, the Secundinii, is one example of a tower tomb, common in Italy, the Rhineland, and several other parts of the Roman world. It stands to its original height, and bears well-executed scenes, now worn, showing members of the family engaged in making and selling cloth as well as mythological subjects connected with a hopeful expectation of the afterlife.

The cost of ·tombs such as these is hard to determine. Study of

Figure 39 The grave monument at Igel, near Trier, set up by members of the Secundinii family

inscriptions from Italy and from African provinces which record how much was spent on the provision of a memorial for their occupants shows that expenditure could range from the lavish to the relatively miserly. The highest recorded price, that of half a million sesterces for a tomb in the Italian town of Fabrateria Nova, is balanced by the 120 sesterces spent by Aurelia Quintina in memory of her husband Aurelius Super at Cremona. It is difficult to translate these prices into modern figures, and perhaps the only judge of how great an expense even the latter figure was is to express it in terms of an annual military salary – figures which can by and large be deduced from existing Roman documentation. Soldiers in the praetorian guard, for example, who were well paid, received 4,000 sesterces a year, and are recorded as having paid anything between 2,000 and 5,000 sesterces for their tombs: these payments may have been augmented due to the hidden insurance benefits payable as a result of membership of a 'burial club' to which the men had contributed during their lifetime. Even so, they show the importance attached by certain classes of society to ensuring that their last resting place was as well provided for as possible, and the obvious lavishness of their decoration demonstrates this too.

Some of the archaeological possibilities of the grave itself having been examined, its relationship to other graves in the neighbourhood can also be investigated. As we have seen, a regular Roman practice was to bury alongside the roads leading out of the settlement; cemeteries at Ostia followed this pattern, but, from the examination of the graves, their dating on grounds of architectural style, and their structural relationships, it is clear that very little control was exercised over the layout of the cemetery by any central authority. In cemeteries where the graves are not marked by architectural constructions or plot boundaries, it may be possible to determine from the plan of the site how the cemetery grew, what was its original size, and, particularly if it is a later Roman and possibly Christian cemetery centred on the tomb of a martyr or bishop, what was its focal point. Study of such interrelationships and patterns of growth will help to determine how earlier graves were treated. If they were set out in regular rows, and no encroachment took place, some degree of planning must have been involved, and the graves probably were marked in some way on the surface – perhaps by stone or wooden markers. This kind of close analysis also can begin to identify groups of family or kinship graves set together within the cemetery, distinguishable from the others by their orientation, their grave furniture, or the evidence they contain for a particular rite of burial. In such ways, the development of the cemetery can begin to be understood through the medium of archaeology.

The careful analysis of graves and the groups of objects found within them, linked to consideration of the plan and layout of the cemetery, will work in two ways; it will enable the date of the establishment of the cemetery to be determined and, in the close grouping of objects in contemporary use (leaving aside those strays which may have been considered heirlooms), can provide a useful cross-check against other dated sequences of material such as pottery or metalwork. The sequence of cremations or inhumations can also be linked with architectural styles, the evidence from the deposited grave-goods being compared with the delineation of different architectural styles evident within the grave monument themselves. All this is of the greatest usefulness, not only in the attempt to understand and closely date evolving styles of pottery, artifacts, and architecture, but also in the assessment of the pattern of changing practice and taste in Roman burials as a whole. This forms part of the sociological picture.

More evidence comes from epigraphy. Tombstones are one of the best sources for information about the career structure of Roman public life, but the information on them can also have other applications. Occasionally, the tombstone will give a glimpse into what individual Romans thought about death and the prospect of an afterlife, or what they were able to express about their grief at the loss of a relative. Many of such expressions may be conventional, and it must therefore be a matter for modern interpretation how much can be read into such evidence. It is a socio-anthropological question whether such carved memorials are evidence of real grief, or whether they represent the expected reaction to a relatively common event at a time when life-expectancy was short.

At all events, the study of epigraphic sources can help to give other, more fundamental data. These can indicate, for example, not only the current names of the populace in a given area, but also, judging from the non-Roman component in the recorded names, the possible size of the foreign or 'native' element in the population. Tombstones, which normally record the age of the deceased, can also give some limited statistics about life-expectancy, and, when their evidence is assembled statistically, may be able to show that men and women had different average life-spans or that their funeral rites or the treatment of their tombs varied according to their sex.

This is all some distance from archaeology in the traditional sense of recording and classifying the material remains, but it serves to point to ways in which elements of archaeological classification or methods of gathering information from the artifacts and sites of the past can be put to maximum use. Archaeologists are constantly improving their understanding of the ancient world by applying a range of techniques borrowed from other disciplines – historical demography, sociology and anthropology, statistics or economics – to their data. When by this means it is able to extract historical or social interpretations, archaeology does not always reveal the picture which might have been obtained had one relied for information on the works of Roman historians or other contemporary accounts.

It is important to remember that these contemporary sources form virtually the only link between archaeological material and the events of Roman history. In dating pottery or jewellery, as we have seen, the search for a well-attested date either for an object's manufacture or for the moment when it was deposited in the ground may focus on a particular historical association. This is a far rarer occurrence, however, than many people might like to think, and many accepted dates for artifacts rely to a greater or lesser extent on a complex network of associations with other material. Their link with 'historical' (that is, recorded) events, if examined carefully, is often tenuous. This does not make the dates assigned to them necessarily false or wrong: but those who use pottery and other artifacts dated by association in this way to give a dated framework to developments at the sites they are studying need constantly to be reminded that such dates are merely the most consistent current explanation of how objects interrelate. It is always possible that further work will make it necessary to adopt new explanations.

Roman archaeology has sometimes been seen in the past as a kind of visual aid to the works of historians or commentators like Livy, Tacitus, or Pliny. As contemporary observers of the historical and political scene, theirs was the unique eye-witness testimony. They tended, however, to ignore the commonplace, and in general failed to describe how things looked. If archaeological finds can in some sense make the impact of their account more immediate by displaying the remains of Pompeii re-emerging from its cover of volcanic ash, this helps to dramatize what was clearly a spectacularly tragic event. Nevertheless, dramatic and poignant though this may be, and a wonderful illustration of Pliny's text, the remains of the buildings and the twisted bodies occasionally discovered within them at Pompeii are only a tiny fragment of the story which archaeological study of the town is able to reveal. Recent research has been concentrating on the origins of the town, its phases of growth, the building development of some of the individual *insulae*, and the complex patterns and sequences which can begin to be revealed by the history of its buildings. Even this is not the full story, for pottery and other artifacts from the site must also have much to tell about the trade-links which the city has established, the relative prosperity of its citizens and the basis of its wealth, as well as revealing aspects of its social and human history. About all this, Pliny tells us little or nothing.

At Pompeii, as at many other Roman sites, this kind of information lies in the ground waiting to be extracted and interpreted by those who are prepared to make use of all the modern means and techniques for gathering it. Far from being merely the handmaid of Roman history, therefore, archaeological study has come very much into its own.

10

The future of Roman archaeology

For archaeology to begin properly to tell its own story of life in the Roman period it is necessary to view its evidence as independently of historical source material as possible. Valid conclusions come from studying all the available evidence – or from ensuring that any sample selected for study is representative enough to give meaningful conclusions about its nature. This can pose something of a dilemma. For practical reasons, much current work and official funding is aimed at salvaging and studying those remains of the past – not just the Roman period – which are directly under threat of elimination by some *force majeure*, whether this is the construction of a new motorway, the effects of annual ploughing on deeply buried remains, the natural forces of erosion on an exposed cliff-top, or any one of a number of other pressures. The archaeological problem comes in reconciling the urgent requirement to respond to pressure of this kind with the challenge of ensuring that any new work provides a supply of fresh data which will contribute significantly to our knowledge of the past.

Most countries in what was once the Roman 'known world' have their own mechanisms, at a national or local level, for funding archaeological work; they have organizational structures, whether nationally or regionally based, for responding by survey or excavation to pressure on areas known to be of historical significance, or for deploying research funds to projects of particular merit or importance. There is thus a continuing record of achievement measured by the advancement of knowledge of the material culture of the Roman empire, and thus aspects of the provincial historical framework. Virtually all are agreed, however, that with continuing constraints upon funding, the major input into archaeological work must go into two main branches – preservation of the remains and necessary examination of them in those cases where their destruction is inevitable.

As we have already seen, the unique nature of excavation, which could be described as the application of archaeological experiment on the remains of buried sites, is that it results in the systematic destruction of the object of its study. In the process, much of the evidence from a site which can help to date it or determine its character is removed, and the site itself may be dismantled so that its structural history can be

155

understood, leaving at the end of the exercise a carefully sifted pile of artifacts together with a record on paper or on photographic film of what the rest of the site looked like. It is of prime importance, therefore, to ensure that sites are not needlessly or aimlessly disturbed. What is most precious is the information that the site contains, which can increasingly be used to build up pictures of the past in ways described in earlier chapters of this book.

Protection and preservation of this resource can be achieved in different ways. One way would be to ensure that none of the common external threats – such as ploughing, afforestation, quarrying, or construction work – is permitted to endanger its physical survival; another would be to seek by excavation and research to record a site under threat of damage or destruction as comprehensively as possible, thus maximizing the information from it in the short term.

The first approach, to ensure that sites are protected from external threat, is a perennial problem where archaeological remains are fragile and vulnerable, or where there are competing demands on a portion of land which contains a site of value. It is neither possible nor necessary to preserve all traces of the Roman past which have survived to this day. In sheer practical terms, one cannot expect to fossilize the centre of some of our major European cities in the cause of archaeological conservation by ensuring that no further or deeper foundations for buildings are sunk into the ground because of the damage they might cause to buried remains. Nor is it feasible to claim that every trace of every field-ditch and enclosure of Roman date observed through the medium of cropmarks on aerial photographs is of such vital importance that farmers should be prevented from ploughing the land which contains them. Gravel extraction companies cannot be expected to cease operations once any traces of such ditches have been spotted within the overburden of gravel which they are currently working. What is required, however, is some analysis of the scale of importance of Roman sites, their value for present-day or future research, an assessment of their character and state of preservation, followed by a sensitive procedure for defining a sample of the most significant sites accompanied by positive steps towards their preservation.

Archaeologists may argue long and hard over how large such a sample should be, which sites it should contain, whether its concentration should be on military or civilian, religious or rural settlement sites. Ideally, however, it should be possible to strike a balance which accords both with the intensity of surviving remains on the ground and with current assessments of their value and importance. Both these factors would have to be kept under review, and if future research were to exhaust the possibilities of one particular type of site, for example, there would be little point in maintaining further examples of the same type on the register of those worth preserving. Conversely, if good examples of particular types of site became disturbed or damaged to such an extent that their archaeological value was seriously impaired, there would be little point in retaining them within the sample, and others of the same type might be substituted in their place. Once established, however, the selected sample of sites would target those which are candidates for positive action to prevent damage or to establish beneficial regimes of management. It needs to be noted, however, that the very existence of such a well-defined sample would not automatically guarantee the necessary funding to protect sites in these ways: that depends in large measure on the goodwill of owners as well as on the political judgements and priorities of those who command the sources of available finance.

It must be asked why it is necessary to preserve sites. In answer, it is not sufficient merely to point to the increased rate of growth of developments in both inner-city and rural areas and estimate the scale of disruption these might cause to archaeological sites of all periods if allowed to run unchecked. There are more positive reasons for preservation than merely the prevention of damage in the short term.

Paramount among these is the concern that the archaeological record – itself the product of man's past activities – is a precious and fragile resource. Like reserves of coal or gas, timber forests or the ozone layer, this may not last for ever, and it must therefore be treated with respect if we are to husband these links with our past and hand them on in an undamaged state to future generations.

There are other, more immediately practical reasons for preservation. First, the scale of archaeological work, and the necessary concentration of effort, not only in the actual excavation and recording of a site, but also in the post-excavation phase when the results are digested, material from the site is studied, and more general conclusions are drawn from it, means that available resources for full-scale examination of sites can only be concentrated in a limited number of places at any one time. It therefore makes sense to ensure, as far as possible, that there is a bank of sites which do not require excavation and can be safely left while the concentration of effort goes on those which most urgently require attention. This, too, has its benefits: for by examining one site at a time, adapting excavation techniques to match particular types of site – with the aim of getting as much information out of the exercise as possible – can be refined and improved. Research questions can be redefined and properly identified by digesting the results from one site before moving on to another, and so on. If there were a complete mêlée of action, accompanied by little thought and strategic planning, the chances of substantially increasing our understanding of the Roman world would be diminished.

Second, the very exercise of selecting sites for preservation helps enormously to focus attention on the scale of past research and on aspects of its practical application for the future. Faced with the request, again somewhat akin to the 'desert island' question, of choosing a sample of Roman forts along the Roman frontiers in Germany for positive preservation, a great deal of the response would have to rely on the scale of past research (as shown in the publications of the Reichslimeskommission as well as more recent research by the relevant Bundesdenkmalamt), the present state of survival of the remains, an assessment of the complexity of individual sites on the frontier, the extent of their relationship with other Roman installations, with civilian settlements and associated *vici* and so on, coupled with a view of the present-day practicalities of preservation. This whole exercise would involve a great deal of sharpening of perspectives, of analysis, and of the formulation of further research questions to be tackled in future work.

Perhaps most importantly, preservation is necessary because of the fundamentally destructive nature of examination of a site by excavation methods. In the last sixty years, since the days when the fort of Richborough was under excavation, there has been an enormous growth in our techniques of exploration, in the retrieval of information of all kinds from excavation work, and in overall expectations of what count as successful results. Professionally speaking, the archaeologist now has a far more impressive battery of skills at his disposal, and a wider range of expertise to call on, than was ever thought possible then. Techniques and applications are improving and increasing in scope all the time, to the extent that it may not be sheer fantasy to think that the most sophisticated recording and information retrieval methods of today may be considered crude and naïve in another sixty years' time. Thus, since the archaeological resource is a finite one, unless we hand down a sufficient body of undisturbed material for our successors to examine, advances in understanding aided by ever better and more refined techniques of study will be impossible.

Not all examination of sites need be destructive, although excavation itself has been described as 'controlled destruction', and its end product is often to transfer the actual three-dimensional site in the ground as far as possible onto two-dimensional paper. Where this is done successfully and objectively, as begun by Pitt-Rivers, succeeding generations have the opportunity to reinterpret sites and finds in the light of their own experience. The increased use of non-destructive techniques to prospect sites may point another way forward: at present aerial, magnetometer, resistivity, and other survey techniques can begin to tell us what is in the ground before the surface is broken by trowel, spade, or JCB. Might not modern technologies eventually afford methods of laser beam or X-ray analysis of undisturbed sites which allow non-destructive methods of examination, and make the destructive art of excavation a thing of the past? If this seems far-fetched, imagine what the reaction of Bushe-Fox, the excavator of Richborough, might have been if he had been told before he began to dig what appeared at the outset to be a level site that he would actually find that there had been a series of triple deep ditches around a central massive monument within the fort walls. Given favourable conditions resistivity survey – had it been available to him – ought to have been able to pick this kind of feature up prior to excavation work.

If preservation is impossible, it is necessary to have recourse to the second option, that of excavation to record the remains of the site before its destruction. Our capability to respond to this kind of emergency may pose further problems, not least that of knowing where best to deploy available resources. At any one time, it is probable that a number of different Roman sites are threatened with destruction or damage. They will not all be of equal importance, and estimates of which are the important ones based, for example, on the degree of survival of buried remains or on how rich or complex the site may be may rely on partial or incomplete evidence. In any case, to some degree our judgement in advance of the kind or quality of information the exploration of any of the sites will reveal may be conditioned by past, and possibly out-of-date, answers to similar questions. If, as is almost invariably the case, financial resources are limited, should one spread relatively small sums around among all the sites under threat, or should one target key sites and effectively write off those adjudged to be of lesser importance, allowing them to be destroyed without record?

The case can be argued both ways: if all sites are examined, at least a partial record can be made of every known Roman site, and the potential of all of them is tested before they are eliminated. However, unless funding can be switched to those which prove on first examination to be of unusual importance, there is a danger that no completely thorough excavation work may in fact take place, and any conclusions will have to be drawn on the basis of a rather imperfect sampling exercise alone. This may greatly distort our understanding of the nature or the history of any one individual site.

Conversely, to be more selective and only to examine those sites which already have proven or suspected real worth lays archaeologists open to the nagging fear that they may have made a wrong decision in allowing the lesser sites to be destroyed without record. In addition, they may be open to the criticism that they are in danger of ignoring the fact that our understanding of the way in which the Roman world worked is impoverished unless we examine and understand the role of lesser sites as well as the most important ones. By allowing examination, too, of only the best attested Roman sites, there is a danger that all further research will be channelled along lines already well established, leaving little scope for new emphases or interpretations.

These opposing views represent perhaps two poles of opinion. In practice, arguments are rarely as clear-cut, and decisions about whether or not to excavate depend upon a number of factors which include the likely benefits from the work in terms of knowledge gained, the adjudged importance of the site from surveys or from trial work, as well as practical considerations such as the nature and urgency of the threat, the availability of the right specialists to undertake the work, and so on. In this way, a balance between pragmatism and academic respectability is sought, though it may not always in everyone's opinion be found.

In view of the destructive nature of archaeological excavation, is there ever good reason to dig a site which is not under threat of destruction? This poses the dilemma of responsibility for the archaeologist: the discipline can only progress through the examination of new sites and the application of new techniques, but the very practice of these – whether productive or not – will virtually unfailingly result in lasting damage to the site, the subject of the exercise. It is clear that the archaeological profession as a whole must demand the highest standards of its practitioners and that anyone who excavates a site must be aware of the responsibility he or she carries. Questions of competence, the levels of past achievement, financial resources, and strategy must be raised, by professionals if no one else, when proposals are put forward for excavation, especially if the site chosen is acknowledged to be of prime importance.

Concentrating excavation work on those sites which are due to be damaged by other pressures which cannot be diverted in a sense removes some of the weight from this argument, since the primary destructive force is not the archaeologist but the less controllable pressure for development or change of one kind or another. In responding to this pressure, the archaeologist is converted at a stroke from a wilful and possibly selfish destructive force – someone who appears to be prepared to sacrifice something irreplaceable in the cause of his or her own scientific research – into a crusader whose intervention before the bulldozers arrive is the only opportunity there is to salvage any precious information at all from a site.

Things in practice are never as starkly black or white. If research excavation on an unthreatened site poses the moral dilemma of destruction in the cause of progress, rescue excavation can pose equally sensitive questions about whether the archaeologist can deliver value for money. The problem can be formulated along these lines: if sites of prime importance are protected from destruction in any case (and therefore do not need excavation), to what extent is it reasonable or indeed feasible to formulate valid questions, test research hypotheses, and make effective use of the funding available on what must by definition be expendable, second-order sites?

Pressure for change makes it impossible to preserve everything – even the very best – of the past, thus sites examined by rescue excavation are not always the second-order ones. No one could claim that in the very important Iron Gates dam project on the River Danube, which flooded many important Roman sites, including Trajan's rock-cut road along the riverside, as well as major prehistoric and other sites (such as Lepenski Vir), affected only the less important sites. Nor could it realistically be claimed that elements of Roman buildings – the Roman forum of London, or the palace of the governor of Lower Germany at Köln – revealed in the centre of some of our most historic cities are of secondary importance. The scale of the threat or the commercial imperative posed by inner-city developments, however, may mean that there has to be a concentration on high-cost, technically difficult urban excavations at the expense of less complex, large-scale rural work. In any case, it could be argued, the costs of excavation and processing of its results are such that it might almost make better economic sense to purchase a rural site outright, and establish a management regime which will be beneficial to its survival, rather than pay the high costs of seeing it excavated prior to ploughing, drainage, or afforestation.

Despite this, it is still possible to argue that the best way of learning more about the Roman past would be to cast off the shackles imposed by the imperatives of rescue archaeology, and concentrate available resources, in terms of excavation and survey techniques, on the analysis of an area of Roman landscape – perhaps that of a Roman *civitas* and its *territorium,* studying villas, agricultural exploitation, industries, small villages, and rural settlements of all types as well as the central focus, the town itself. To be really effective, this would have to be as complete and exhaustive a survey as possible, making full use of field-walking, aerial photography, and sampling techniques, and taking every opportunity offered for examination of Roman structures or features, buildings as well as field systems. Eventually, by compiling a picture of how the *civitas* unit worked socially and economically, what were the prevailing agricultural practices, climate, flora and fauna, the numbers, the physiological characteristics, and the ethnic affinities of the population, a complete and valuable piece of the jigsaw pattern which is the Roman empire would become available. Whilst this is undoubtedly the aim of current research in many areas, it could be argued that only by applying considerable resources into one or two specifically selected areas for this treatment will comprehensible results begin to emerge in even the medium term. Even so, the problems of where to select would be immense, as would the losses of information in other areas which had not been selected for this treatment.

Part of the answer to the question how archaeologists reach their conclusions about material from the past must therefore spring from the use of resources in obtaining material for study. Effective information-gathering can only be achieved by posing the right questions of the site which is to be examined, by structuring the deployment of resources to maximize the information return from the work, and by a correct blending of necessity and opportunism which not only calls forth an archaeological response in the first place, but which is also the hallmark of a competent excavation director. If an excavation project is not well conceived at the outset, it is unlikely that any of the bewildering battery of scientific and multidisciplinary approaches to the data it produces will bear much fruit.

Another part is, of course, interpretation. It may be thought that in applying modern and relatively sophisticated techniques to archaeological data something of the romance and the expert specialization inherent in subjective interpretation is lost. Proper archaeological interpretation, however, while it may be part inspirational, must rely upon a clear understanding and appreciation of all the available facts. Speculation on the reasons for observed data, and some theorizing beyond this, which may allow new ideas to be thrown up which can be tested by the results of future archaeological work, is a natural way to push the subject forward. There is always a place for inspired interpretation. This has to be kept firmly within the bounds of the possible and within the limitations of the evidence if only in order for it not to be branded as part of archaeology's 'lunatic fringe'.

Archaeological work has its romance. It allows us to get close to people of the past, and in a sense to identify with them. There is a directness about the soldier's shoes or the leather bikini recovered from the waterlogged mud at the bottom of a well, the spout cup and the set of clay figures from a child's grave, and the writing-tablet which invites a friend to a birthday party. These are all artifacts which were worn, used, or handled by real people, and if just by being there they manage to tell us something about the way of life of those past owners, so much the better. Our response is not to deny the undoubted appeal of this kind of human understanding across the centuries, but to accept that the physical fabric of such artifacts can also be revealing.

We cannot avoid putting our own contemporary interpretation on Roman material. The Roman sculpture of a squirrel and a mouse may be in our view charming; what response would it have called forth to its contemporaries? We may find it relatively easy to gloss over the barbarity of Roman times, the cheapness of life, the rigid stratification into a class society. One has only to think of Roman historians' accounts of shows put on in the amphitheatre, of the exposure of new-born babies, or of the treatment of slaves to remember that life was a great deal more brutal for most people then than now. Study of the archaeological record should allow this to be seen more dispassionately, not in the sort of personal detail in which individual historians will have recorded it, but in more general ways – the wear and tear on bodies in the cemeteries, the amount of vermin in the streets, the indicators of economic growth or decline in industries or communities. It will never tell us what the individual Roman felt about the death of a loved relative or about the economics of the Spanish wine-trade, or about his taste in interior decoration. It will, however, tell us how carefully a body was laid out for burial, allow us to estimate the volume of wine reaching Rome from Spain, or show us floor mosaics of exquisite workmanship, some with quotations from the classics.

What, then, is the way forward? Will there come a stage when information-gathering about specific sites must stop – as it did for the German frontier commission in the 1920s and 1930s pending the absorption of the results and the formulation of new questions to be answered? Will it be possible to maintain a healthy marriage between rescue and research – or should a greater emphasis be put onto research excavation on unthreatened sites in order to answer new questions and provide new data? Is it right to use available funds to support the gathering of information over a wide front, at many different sites in most of the major Roman provinces? Would better results, in terms of our understanding of the Roman economic and social structure, be obtained if resources were concentrated on the major and comprehensive examination of a single Roman town or city together with its surrounding Roman landscape? If this were to be an agreed strategy, could we be prepared to countenance seeing a number of other sites (perhaps of an importance equal to those under study within our chosen area) destroyed without record in the cause of concentrating efforts in this way? How, too, could such a strategy be implemented, entailing as it might enormous problems of international agreement and co-operation, and serious implications for the deployment of resources away from existing channels and into new ones?

These are perhaps dangerous areas of speculation, but such considerations help to invigorate debate about what archaeologists of the Roman period are trying to achieve. Much has been learned in recent years from techniques of study applied to sites and excavated material from other periods, where there exists no ready-made historical framework in which it can be set. The way forward, whatever path it may actually take, must allow archaeological evidence to tell its own story and to make the direct contribution which it can to the study of the Roman past; it must not merely be regarded as the 'handmaid of history'. It must continue to challenge accepted doctrines, to develop new methods of research, and to provoke new avenues of inquiry. The experience of archaeology can be satisfying, but we can never be satisfied that it is complete.

Index

References to figures are in italic

Adam, Robert 22
aerial photography 41–2, 99–102, 131, 156
Africa 100, 121, 123
Agricola 34
Agrippa 5, 79
Albinus, Clodius 40
Alcantara 63
Alcubierre 10–11
Allectus 40
Ammianus Marcellinus 40–1
Antium, battle of 4
Antonine Itinerary 10, 55
Antonine Wall 40
Aquileia 44
archaeology: conclusions from 58–9; dating from 50–2, 56–9, 72–3; definition 49–51; geographical techniques 147–8; and history 40, 48–62, 155, 163; methods of 52–3; and other techniques 144–54; profession of 42–3, 46–7, 105–7; responsibility 160; rural 92–6, 131–2; and sampling 145; and statistics 144–5
Ardoch 92
Arrian 55
art treasures 4, 7, 14–15, 21–2
artifacts 109–26, 144–5; dating from 110, 112–19, 154; functions of 109; *see also* brooches, coins, glassware, jewellery, pottery
Arundel, Earl of 10
Athens 5, 15
Aurelian 73
Ausonius 55

Autun 6, 63

Baalbek 26–7, 41
Barcelona 63
Bede 7
Belgrade 90
Benwell 17
Bersu, Gerald 39
Birdoswald 34, *35*, 128
Blackstone Edge 1
Blondus, Flavius 6
bones 52, 127; animal 131–3; bird 133; human 133–4
Bonn 90
Bramante 7
brick 72–3, 124
Britain 1, 7–8, 22, 29, 39, 42, 44, 46, 92, 131, 136
brooches 52, 148
Bruce, Collingwood 19, 27
Brunelleschi 6
Brünnow 41
Bucharest 90
Budapest 90
buildings: archaeological study of 63–88; dating of 72–4, 112–19; function and form 65–7, 72; and patronage 75
Burg-bei-Stein 72
Bürgle 39
burials 148–53; cremations 149; inhumations 148–9; *see also* cemeteries, tombs
Burlington, Lord 9–10
Burnswark 92, 94
Bushe Fox, Sir J.P. 35, 158